BRIGHT LEGACY

Bright Legacy

*Portraits of Ten Outstanding
Christian Women*

Edited by
Ann Spangler

SERVANT BOOKS
Ann Arbor, Michigan

Published by Servant Books
P.O. Box 8617
Ann Arbor, Michigan 48107

Cover photo by John B. Leidy © 1983
by Servant Books
Jacket & book design by John B. Leidy

Printed in the United States of America
ISBN 0-89283-167-7

Contents

Acknowledgments

EXCERPTS from the following books are gratefully acknowledged. They have been used by permission of the publisher.

The Helper; copyright © 1978 by Catherine Marshall. Published by Chosen Books, Lincoln, Virginia 22078.
Meeting God at Every Turn; copyright © 1980 by Catherine Marshall LeSourd. Published by Chosen Books, Lincoln, Virginia 22078.
To Live Again; copyright © 1957 by Catherine Marshall. Published by Chosen Books, Lincoln, Virginia 22078.

The poems of Wilma Burton are reprinted with permission of her estate.

The poems of Elizabeth Rooney are copyright © Elizabeth Rooney and reprinted here with permission.

Quotations from the works of Amy Carmichael are taken from copyrighted material and used by permission of the Christian Literature Crusade, Fort Washington, Pennsylvania 19034.

Unless otherwise noted photographs have been provided by the courtesy of the authors.

Contributors

✍ **Elisabeth Elliot** is the author of *Discipline: The Glad Surrender, Through Gates of Splendor, Let Me Be a Woman, Love Has a Price Tag, The Savage My Kinsman,* and many other books. Her first husband, Jim Elliot, along with four other missionaries, was speared to death by Auca Indians in Ecuador. She currently resides with her husband Lars Gren in Massachusetts.

✍ **Gladys Hunt** is the author of *Honey for a Child's Heart, Ms. Means Myself,* and several Fisherman Bible Study Guides. She and her husband Keith are associated with Inter-Varsity Christian Fellowship.

✍ **Kathryn Koob** was one of two women held hostage in Iran during the U.S. Embassy takeover from November 1979 to January 1981. Awarded a Medal of Valor from the United States Government, she tells her story in *Guest of the Revolution.*

✍ **Madeleine L'Engle** is a prolific author. Her best-known books include *A Wrinkle in Time, A Wind in the Door, A Swiftly Tilting Planet,* and *The Summer of the Great Grandmother.* She is married to Hugh Franklin, an actor on ABC's *All My Children.*

✍ **Karen Burton Mains** is the author of *Open Heart, Open Home; The Key to a Loving Heart; Karen! Karen!* and *The Fragile Curtain.* The mother of four children, she frequently joins her husband David on radio broadcasts of Chapel of the Air.

✍ **Kitty Muggeridge** collaborated on a life of her aunt, the celebrated Beatrice Webb. She has translated *La Fontaine's Fables* from the French as well as *The Sacrament of the Present Moment* by Jean Pierre de Caussade. She is the wife of Malcolm Muggeridge, well-known on both sides of the Atlantic as one of the most perceptive social critics of our time.

◇ **Rebecca Manley Pippert** is the author of *Out of the Saltshaker: Evangelism as a Way of Life.* She is married to Wesley Pippert, a reporter for United Press International.

◇ **Luci Shaw** is the author of *The Sighting; Colossians: Focus on Christ;* and *Listen to the Green.* She and her husband Harold own and operate Harold Shaw Publishers.

◇ **Elizabeth Sherrill** has collaborated with her husband John on *The Hiding Place, The Cross and the Switchblade, God's Smuggler,* and several other books. She is an editor of Chosen Books and *Guideposts* magazine.

◇ **Ingrid Trobisch** is the author of *On Our Way Rejoicing* and co-author with her late husband Walter of *My Beautiful Feeling: Letters to Ilona.*

Preface

EACH PERSON ENTERS LIFE with an inheritance, a legacy, if you will. Listen to the family's remarks when a baby comes home from the hospital. His dimpled chin looks just like Uncle Harold's. Her long, delicate fingers are exactly like her sister Ellen's. I once knew a child who was fondly dubbed "Winston Churchill" by loving parents and friends. The child's stubby nose, wrinkled brow, and serious face lacked only a cigar to complete the resemblance.

In truth, each of us arrives in this world with certain characteristics inherited from our parents and their parents before them. This inheritance profoundly shapes our life and identity. And in these things we have no choice.

But there is another legacy that does come to us by choice. It is the Christian legacy, the inheritance that becomes ours when we give our lives to Christ and are called by his name. Even so, it is a legacy which comes to us now only in part. It is a promise not fully realized until the life to come. Meanwhile, as St. Paul says, we "press on toward the goal for the prize of the upward call of God in Christ Jesus."

Part of this striving, this pressing on toward the goal, involves the struggle to become better persons, bright beacons to penetrate the darkness that threatens to envelop the world around us. It will help us in this struggle to look for real people, fellow Christians who though flawed in heart and mind have nonetheless given their all to God and emerged as individuals who can light the way ahead. It is simply good sense to learn from other Christians about the perils that face us and the rewards that await us. It can be tremendously encouraging to realize from their example that we can succeed—and succeed gloriously—despite the obstacles.

With this in mind I posed the following question to each of the contributors to this book: "Would you write about someone you particularly admire, a woman remarkable for her generosity, love, and faithfulness?" The response was enthusiastic—and varied. The

1

contributors have written chapters about missionaries, authors, an English governess, a mother, a Swedish grandmother, an heiress, and the wife of a hero of the American Revolution. Many of these women lived challenging lives as wives and mothers. Some of them struggled with poverty, were thrown into jail, or spent most of their lives as missionaries on foreign soil, thousands of miles from home. But as varied as the circumstances of these women were, their lives of courage, love, and faithfulness speak powerfully of the One they followed.

This is not to imply that they were perfect people. On the contrary. Each of these women had to contend against external and internal obstacles—their own pride, stubbornness, discouragement, and doubts. But through it all God has made them better women, stronger Christians, true women of influence.

Dwight Moody said, "Character is what you are in the dark." Certainly many of the women faced the darkest circumstances, and the contributors have not tried to hide the dark or to magnify the light in the lives of the women they write about. Their goal was only to tell the truth. As a result, we learn not only about the women whose stories they tell but also about the authors themselves—their hopes, struggles, and deepest ideals. As Rebecca Pippert puts it, "The underlying assumption of this book is that in addition to needing heroes and role-models we must be ones for others."

This, then, is the inheritance we share, that bright legacy which we receive and, through the grace of God, pass on to others.

ANN SPANGLER

Courtesy *Our Sunday Visitor*

Mother Teresa of Calcutta

by Kitty Muggeridge

S HE WAS TINY and her white sari, edged with blue, framed a shrewd face with a mischievous smile and serious grey eyes. She spoke of love and suffering in the slums of Calcutta and of meeting Jesus there. When she was not speaking herself, she listened humbly, her head bent, her hands folded, her eyes closed as though in prayer. It was 1967 and Mother Teresa was being interviewed on BBC television by my husband Malcolm.

At first, he said, the tape was considered unimpressive and disappointing. However, when it was shown on a Sunday evening, the response was immediate and enthusiastic. "It was greater than I have ever known to any comparable programme," he wrote later on. "Both in mail and in contributions of money for Mother Teresa's work; from young and old, rich and poor, educated and uneducated. All of them said approximately the same thing: 'This woman spoke to me as no one ever has and I feel I must help her.'" Mother Teresa had captivated her audience. "She has no exceptional gift of eloquence or charisma," Malcolm explained. "It might indeed be said that her ordinariness itself was a kind of rare beauty, as her homilies are, in their simplicity and sincerity, a kind of rare eloquence."

Although this was her first public appearance in the West, she had been known for some years in India for her work among the poor of Calcutta. The success of this first television appearance in England led to the BBC arranging for the television producer, Peter Chafer, to go to Calcutta with Malcolm to make a film of her work there. "We will do something beautiful for God," she said, thus providing the title. The temple of Kali, the Hindu Goddess, renamed the House of the Dying, where Mother Teresa and her sisters brought the sick and dying in off the streets, was so dark that the cameraman, Ken MacMillan, insisted that there could be no question of filming there. However, he was persuaded to have a try, taking, as a precaution, shots of some of the sick people lying outside the temple. When the film was processed, the shots in the temple were bathed in a beautiful soft light and the shots outside appeared blurred and unuseable. No one could account for it. Ken, a sceptic, could not believe his eyes. As often with Mother Teresa, God had done something beautiful for her. A miracle had happened. Later, the book *Something Beautiful for God* was published. The author cannot remember taking any part in writing it except that he held the pen. The words were Mother Teresa's. But she herself says that she is only "a little pencil in God's hands," which must be the reason why this slender volume has been translated into many foreign languages and has continued to earn money for her work. Since then, many miracles have happened.

Mother Teresa was born in 1910 in Yugoslavia and christened Gonxha. She had one sister, Aga, born in 1905, and one brother, Lazar, two years younger then herself and now her only living close relative. Her parents, Nicola and Dronda Bojaxhui, were Albanians who settled in Skopijé, a town in a part of Albania annexed by Yugoslavia in 1909. Her father was a merchant builder and an Albanian nationalist, active in the prevailing political strife, fighting on the side dedicated to restoring independence for his country. Her mother was a pious Catholic at a time when the majority of the population was Moslem; the rest were Greek Orthodox except for a tiny Catholic minority. She brought up her family in strict accord with Catholic principles. And together they took part in the various activities of their church.

The Bojaxhuis were a happy, prosperous family, full of love and joy until one day in 1919. Nicola Bojaxhui, then forty-six years old, came home one evening from work in acute pain. He was rushed to a hospital, but nothing could be done and he died a few hours later. His son believes that he was poisoned by his political enemies.

After that, the family's fortune changed radically and Dronda was left with the task of bringing up her young family alone and of making financial provision for them and for herself. She soon started a business, with the help of her children after school hours, which dealt in rugs, embroideries, and all manner of handicrafts.

From then on the family became even more involved in their church, and little Gonxha spent every spare moment at the Jesuit headquarters in the parish. This is how her brother describes his young sister at age nine: "She was plump, round, tidy, sensible, and a little too serious for her age. Of the three of us, she alone did not steal jam." She and her sister Aga were both very musical and enjoyed singing in the choir. But what Gonxha loved most was to listen to the missionaries from India recounting stories of their work in the field.

It was about the time of her twelfth birthday that she first felt called to become a missionary. She said nothing about this at the time and continued studying until she completed high school. Then, at eighteen she confided in her mother. Despite her dismay at the thought of losing her daughter, Dronda Bojaxhui agreed that she could not object if it was truly God's will. But her brother, by now a lieutenant in the Albanian army, was shocked to hear that his pretty, lively, mischievous sister had decided to become a nun. "How could you?" he wrote. "A little girl like you become a nun? Do you realise you are burying yourself?"

Her answer shocked him even more. "You think you are so important as an officer serving a king of two million subjects. Well, I am serving the king of the whole world. Which one of us is right?" To others she said simply: "I could never face God if I didn't do this work."

The parish priest, whose order was related to the Loreto sisters, was impressed by this devout young girl's resolve to become a nun, and it was through him that Gonxha was admitted to the

Congregation of Loreto Nuns in Bengal. First she was sent to the Loreto Abbey in Rathfarnham, near Dublin, where she arrived January 29, 1928. She stayed there for barely two months to learn English before going on to Bengal. She found herself in austere surroundings, unable to understand a word of English. Life at the abbey was far different than the life she had led in her native Yugoslavia. Mother Teresa admits that the only thing she remembers of her stay in Rathfarnham was the dining room. Some of the nuns who were her contemporaries remember the small, shy postulant who had trouble making herself understood. One nun recalls that the only remarkable thing about her was that she was so ordinary.

On January 29 Gonxha reached India to begin her novitiate with the Loreto sisters in Darjeeling, sometimes known as the City of Lightning. Here the well-to-do would come with their families to escape the stifling heat of a summer in the plains. The convent was a magnificent building, located at the foot of Kanchenjunga, far removed from the poverty the young nun had expected to find. Here she spent two years as a novice until, on May 24, 1931, she took her first vows, choosing the name Teresa, after the "little one not the big one" she insists, meaning Thérèse of Lisieux not Teresa of Avila.

Having completed her novitiate, Sister Teresa was sent to the Loreto Convent in Calcutta, another fine building, surrounded by beautiful grounds in the select district of Entally. Here she taught history and geography for seventeen years in St. Mary's School. This school was run by the nuns and catered to the daughters of the moneyed families. On May 17, 1937, she took her final vows. Eventually, she became the principal of the school as well as head of the Daughters of St. Anne, a congregation of Indian nuns who taught in a Bengali school for girls.

Sister Teresa's room overlooked the slums of Motijeel, and from her window she would often gaze down into the crowded streets. One day in August 1946, she descended into those dark alleys. Standing amid the squalor, poverty, and suffering, she realized that her role lay not as a teacher in the select school for English-speaking girls but here in the slums to live among the poorest of the poor. "I knew where I belonged," she says, "but I didn't know how to reach it."

And then the day came when Sister Teresa heard a second call from God. On September 10, 1946, a day now celebrated by the Missionaries of Charity as "Inspiration Day," Sister Teresa was on her way to Darjeeling, when she heard what she describes as a "call within a call." She was being called to another form of service. "I was to leave Loreto and help the poor while living among them. It was an order. To fail would have been to break faith." She has admitted since "that it was much more difficult to leave Loreto than to leave my family. Loreto, my work, my spiritual training meant everything to me."

Realizing that some medical experience would be essential in her new role, she went off to Patna to take a short course in nursing and dispensary under the direction of the medical missionaries there. Her intention was to start a congregation of sisters who would live like the poorest of the poor, on a diet of rice and salt. They would be allowed to eat what was necessary—nothing more.

Before she was allowed to leave Loreto, permission had to be obtained from the Archbishop of Calcutta for her to live outside the convent and create a new order. Such a request was unlikely to meet with success at any time, but now, on the eve of Indian independence, there were doubts as to whether a European Christian nun working in the slums would be accepted by the Bengal authorities. She had to wait for two years before permission was granted in 1948.

Mother Teresa, founder of the Congregation of the Missionaries of Charity, was thirty-eight years old when she set out alone from the Loreto convent, wearing the now famous white cotton sari, edged with blue and designed by herself, to begin her new work. Thousands of refugees from Pakistan had been driven into Calcutta as a result of the partition of India which took place when the British left in 1947. It was not easy to launch out alone on this challenging new venture into the crowded, poverty-stricken slums. Trudging for miles in search of a home for herself and her sisters to be, Mother Teresa was tempted to abandon her resolve by thoughts of the comfortable life she had left behind. But she never looked back. It was God's will—she must obey.

While continuing her search for a home, she lodged with the Little Sisters of the Poor. Anxious to begin her new work, she rented a hovel in a deserted garden in the slums of Motijeel for five rupees a month and opened a school. Here she taught reading and writing to the children who came in off the streets. With no equipment of any kind, kneeling on the bare ground, she traced out words with a stick. When lessons were over, she made off to the poverty-stricken districts to tend the sick and comfort the dying. At length, through the generosity of Michael Gomes, a Catholic friend, she was lent the use of rooms in his large house in Creek Lane, where she received her first postulant, Sister Agnes, a former student at Loreto. Soon after, ten more followed, all of them former pupils.

In 1950 the Pope approved of the constitution of the Missionaries of Charity, drawn up by Mother Teresa. By this time the congregation had grown so rapidly that there was no longer any room for them in the house in Creek Lane. Father Henry, a Roman Catholic priest, helped them find a house at 54a Lower Circular Road. They were able to buy the house because of the generosity of the Archbishop of Calcutta, who, on the security of faith alone, lent them the money. At last, they were able to settle into a home of their own, a home which was to become their Mother House. For Mother Teresa, fully aware that many priests and nuns had been refused authorization to found their own order, all of this was a miracle.

The aim of the new congregation was "to quench the thirst of Jesus Christ on the Cross." Above the crucifix in every chapel of the Missionaries of Charity are the words "I Thirst." Those aspiring to join the order are required to observe four vows. To follow Christ with undivided love in chastity and in total obedience. To love unconditionally without seeking returns or results. To love in chastity and in a spirit of total surrender. To love in poverty. Poverty is an expression of love; it means total dependence on the will of God. In obedience the Missionaries of Charity dedicate to their Lord their own will, as Christ did, who saved men through his obedience to the will of his Father. The fourth vow, to offer wholehearted, free service to the poorest of the poor, is special to the order.

The sisters observe their vows enthusiastically, living as the poor live, eating no more than they do, owning the barest necessities—a thin mattress, a pair of sandals, two cotton saris, underwear, and a pail to wash in. The one exception is the crucifix pinned to their left shoulder as a reminder of the sacrificial love of Jesus suffering on the cross. "Poverty," says Mother Teresa, "is our only safeguard. We do not want to begin by serving the poor only to end up by unconsciously serving the rich. . . . In order to understand and help those who have nothing we must live like them."

The day begins for the sisters at 4:30 in the morning with Mass followed by a half hour of meditation and morning prayer. Prayers continue in the afternoon, followed in the evening by a full hour of adoration. Echoing the words of St. Paul, Mother Teresa tells her sisters that they must see Jesus and love him in all people. The more repugnant the person, the greater must be their faith, love, and cheerful devotion in ministering to the Lord, however distressing his disguise. They are also enjoined to laugh. "Laughter is a way of communicating joy, and joy is a net of love by which we can catch souls." This is the spirit in which the nuns trip off smiling to run about the dark, squalid slums, to tend the sick and dying and bathe the maggot-infested sores of emaciated bodies. They have become known by some as the running nuns.

When Mother Teresa first moved into the new home, it seemed too big. But the congregation was expanding rapidly, and soon it was filled with new postulants and sister houses were being opened in many parts of India.

Already, in Calcutta, bridge-playing mem-sahibs and high-caste Indian ladies were leaving their elegant drawing rooms to join the sisters in their work among the poor and destitute and the outcast untouchables. By 1954, refugees were pouring into the town from East Pakistan. Hospitals and prisons were dangerously over-crowded; starving families made their homes on station platforms; the dead and dying lay about the streets; children and lepers picked their way among them, scavenging for food. But Mother Teresa and her sisters went out each morning, smiling their way through the filth, picking babies, dead and alive, out of dustbins, rescuing the abandoned and desitute to bring them to the deserted temple of Kali, the home for the dying which the health authorities had already made available for them. The old Hindu monks were not happy about this. One of them who had tried to get the sisters out told the monks: "I promised I would get these women out of the temple and I shall . . . but . . . I shall not get them out of this place before your mothers and sisters do the work these nuns are doing."

The sisters continued to bring the sick and dying either to be tenderly nursed back to health or to draw their last breath, held in loving arms, closing their eyes on a smiling human face. Hindu, Moslem, Buddhist, Catholic and Protestant alike are helped to die in peace with God, "like Angels."

Mother Teresa dispels all fear of death. "Dying is just going home to God," she says. She was asked once to pray for the late Barbara Ward, who was mortally ill. "Your name is up on the wall," she wrote, "and the whole house will pray for you, including me. St. Peter will be surprised at the avalanche of prayers for you and will, I'm sure, make you well again soon. Maybe, though, you are ready to go home to God. If so, he will be very happy to open the door for you and let you in for eternity. P.S. If you do go home before me, give Jesus and His Mother my love." Who would not look forward joyfully to such a welcome?

In 1963, the Congregation of the Missionary Brothers was formed, headed by Brother Andrew, a Jesuit, and the House of the Dying was handed over to them. Some of the work done was considered more suited to men than to women, but the new order has always remained closely associated with the sisters.

In 1955 the first of many children's homes, Shishu Bhavan, was opened, close to the Mother House in Circular Road, which became the refuge for unwanted babies, abandoned waifs, and starving children brought by mothers who had no food for them. None were refused, none died uncared for or unloved. Many grew up to be adopted or fostered. In the film *Something Beautiful for God*, Mother Teresa is seen holding a tiny human curved in the palm of her hand. "See," she cries exultantly, "there's life in her!" The assumptions of over-population are nonsensical to her and she refuses to countenance abortion.

The sisters had already installed a group of lepers on some unused railway property from which the authorities were ashamed to expel them. Their first leper colony, Shantinagar, was officially opened in 1957, and a fund was started to support it. The collection boxes were inscribed with these words: "Touch a leper with your compassion." Someone remarked: "I wouldn't touch a leper for a thousand pounds." Mother Teresa's prompt reply was: "Neither would I. But I would be willing to touch him for the love of God."

Politics are irrelevant for Mother Teresa. "There are those," she says, "who struggle for justice in the world and for human rights and try to change structures. . . . Our mission is to look at the problem individually. If a person feels that God wants him to pledge for the collective change of the social structures, this is a question between him and God." For her, revolution "comes from God and is made of love." Mother Teresa is not a woman who judges others. The harshest comment she ever makes about even the most villainous person is that she has met "Jesus in a *very* distressing disguise." And so the Missionaries of Charity have opened houses in the third world, among the victims of want and despair, and in the West, among the victims of consumerism who are suffering from surfeit and in even greater need of their loving care. They have also opened houses in communist countries such as East Germany and Yugoslavia, and in South America, and, indeed, in countries all over the world. The one exception is Belfast, Northern Ireland, where, after a short stay, the sisters were asked to leave. As it happened, Mother Teresa, as always on the lookout for where her sisters might be needed, had just applied for permission from Haile Selassie for her Missionaries of Charity to work in Ethiopia, which was suffering from a disastrous drought at the time. Before this was granted, she was asked these questions:

"What do you want from the Government?"

"Nothing. I have only come to offer my sisters to work among the poorest suffering people."

"What will your sisters do?"

"We give wholehearted free service to the poorest of the poor."

"What qualifications do you have?"

"We try to bring tender love and compassion to the unwanted and the unloved."

"I see you have quite a different approach. Do you preach to the people, trying to convert them?"

"Our work of love reveals to the suffering poor the love of God for them."

In the short interview that followed, the eighty-year-old Emperor's response was: "I have heard about the good work you do. I am very happy you have come. Yes, let your sisters come to Ethiopia."

So Mother Teresa was able to write to her workers in Belfast, telling them that through the intervention of divine providence the sisters who were excluded from Ireland were now to go to Ethiopia to "feed the hungry Christ . . . [to give] His love and compassion to the suffering people of Ethiopia."

It was now evident that outside help was needed to administer the internationally established convents of the Missionaries of Charity. This was especially the case if the sisters were to continue their life of prayer and meditation, as essential a part of their rule as "feeding the hungry for Christ" in the form of the sick and suffering. For this purpose, a secular branch of the Missionaries of Charity was set up to manage business affairs and organize the collection and distribution of the many gifts and donations arriving daily. One suggestion for the name of the group was the Friends of Mother Teresa. No, Mother Teresa did not want friends, she wanted workers. Finally, the name of Co-Workers was chosen, an expression which Mahatma Ghandi had applied to his helpers.

Accordingly, in 1969, The Association of Co-Workers was formed. It is now under the chairmanship of Mrs. Anne Blaikie, one of the very first helpers in the early days in Calcutta. Mother Teresa, however, does not consider the Co-Workers merely an association concerned with management and organization. She urges them to avoid spending too much time on fund-raising. If it is God's will, he will supply the money they need. They are not like social workers, laboring for a cause. They are working for a person.

Because they belong to God, their work is not an end but a means whereby they can put their love into action, seeing Christ in every person they touch because he has said: "I was hungry, I was thirsty, I was naked, I was sick, I was lonely and you took me." They are a "family united in their purpose to come closer to God and one another through prayer and loving service to their fellow men."

Mother Teresa's whole being is suffused with the beauty of holiness, which she shares in common with all saints. She also possesses what might be called the logic of holiness and the humor of holiness. When the two are combined, they have an irresistible power of persuasion.

For example, when her first novitiate was about to open in England, Mother Teresa invited Cardinal Heenan to open it, giving it his blessing. She wrote to him, saying that she knew he was a very busy man with many important engagements. Even so, she hoped he would come, as Jesus would be there. He came. He had to.

Then again, her brother Lazar recalls a trip he made to the Rome airport to say goodbye to Mother Teresa and her sisters, who were returning to Calcutta. He found them surrounded by a pile of bundles and brown paper parcels, bursting with everything they had collected to take back to the poorest of the poor. Excited officials were standing over them, frantically waving their arms about and flatly refusing to allow the baggage to be taken on the plane. The nuns were paying no attention. Their heads were bowed, their eyes closed, their hands folded in prayer. Presently up came another set of officials, who with resigned shrugs agreed to let the baggage through. Lazar asked his sister what they were praying about. "We were asking God to send other officials," she replied.

He also tells of the time when one of the sisters was in a state of great agitation on account of the theft of a large sum of money. Mother Teresa made no fuss. "Why worry? The money doesn't matter. That is not important. Nobody has stolen you. That would have been something to worry about!"

Mother Teresa always speaks with utmost simplicity. On one occasion she confronted the famous French geneticist, Jack

Monod, on Canadian television. While Monod expounded his faith in genes, Mother Teresa, as is her custom, sat quietly meditating. When he had come to the end of his testimony she was asked what she had to say. Replying to the wisdom of science with the wisdom of holiness she replied: "I believe in love and compassion." The professor left the studio muttering that if he saw more of that woman he'd be in bad trouble. He is now dead, and certainly Mother Teresa will have said a prayer for him.

Many books have been written and many anecdotes told about this amazing nun. She travels far and wide installing new houses and receiving homage from heads of state and those in high places, always returning home with joy and relief to be once again with the poor and suffering, whom she loves. She has appeared on television everywhere, has won nearly every known award, and has established convents in many countries. While other orders have relaxed their rules and found it difficult to attract new members, her convents, with their strict rules of poverty and discipline, are overflowing with novices. Mother Teresa's vast organization of sisters, with branches all over the world, is administered without offices or equipment of any kind and with no overhead. Mother Teresa contradicts in word and deed every cherished fantasy and lie of the twentieth-century consensus, fostered by the media in an overwhelmingly materialistic age. Most remarkable of all, while she is hailed by one and all as a saint, neither media publicity nor worldwide praise have falsified or devalued the sublime truth of her words.

Despite her indifference to fame and her deep humility and total surrender to God, she by no means lacks sound business sense. In 1964, when the Pope presented her with the white Lincoln Continental convertible in which he had been touring India, she knew exactly what to do with it. It was obviously unsuitable for her sisters to drive around the slums in; sold second-hand it would not fetch much, so she held a raffle and collected half a million rupees.

Mother Teresa loves to pray. She lives by prayer. Her favorite, and the one which best expresses the aims of her order, is the prayer attributed to St. Francis of Assisi. It is repeated each day by the Missionaries of Charity:

Lord, make me an instrument of your peace,
Where there is hatred, let me sow love.
Where there is injury, pardon,
Where there is doubt, faith;
Where there is despair, hope;
Where there is darkness, light;
Where there is sadness, joy.
O divine Master, grant that I may not
So much seek to be consoled as to console;
To be understood as to understand;
To be loved as to love;
For it is in giving that we receive;
It is pardoning that we are pardoned;
And it is in dying that we are born to eternal life.

She has also written many prayers herself:

Dearest Lord, may I see you today and every day in the person of your sick, and, whilst nursing them, minister unto you. Though you hide yourself behind the unattractive disguise of the irritable, the exacting, the unreasonable, may I still recognize you, and say: "Jesus, my patient, how sweet it is to serve you."

Lord, help us to see in your crucifixion and resurrection an example of how to endure and seemingly to die in the agony and conflict of daily life, so that we may live more fully and creatively. You accepted patiently and humbly the rebuffs of human life, as well as the tortures of your crucifixion and passion. Help us to accept the pains and conflicts that come to us each day as opportunities to grow as people and become more like you. Enable us to go through them patiently and bravely, trusting that you will support us. Make us realize that it is only by frequent deaths of ourselves and our self-centered desires that we can come to live more fully; for it is only by dying with you that we can rise with you.

These words speak of the intent of her soul, and we listen to them.

Mother Teresa has become a legendary figure. Her role in the world today is beautifully described in the foreword to *A Gift for God*: "God never leaves us in total darkness, at all times and in all circumstances, by one means or another, the alternative to the dreadful assumptions and devices of godless men get demonstrated. Thus, just when it looks as though power is truly the only dynamic in a lost world, a Mother Teresa crops up, with no worldly resources, no special gifts of eloquence or charisma, to assert the dynamic of love. And all the world, instead of ridiculing her and rejecting her, falls in love with her."

In December 1979, the Nobel Prize Committee awarded the Nobel Prize for Peace to Mother Teresa. When her name was first put up the response was: "What has this woman done for peace?" The question is best answered by Mother Teresa herself in her Nobel Lecture, a shortened version of which is quoted below, when, after some delay, she finally won the award.

Having requested beforehand that the usual banquet should not be held and that the money which would have been spent on it be used to feed the hungry, she addressed her distinguished audience, which included the King of Norway. Her brother Lazar was there too. He had come up from Italy to join in the tribute being paid to his famous sister, about whom he had been so mistaken years ago. She spoke simply with her usual unsophisticated eloquence which went straight to the heart of her listeners.

"As we have gathered here together to thank God for the Nobel Peace Prize, I think it will be beautiful that we pray the prayer of St. Francis of Assisi which always surprises me very much and I always wonder that 400 or 500 years ago when St. Francis of Assisi composed it they had the same difficulties that we have today. As we compose this prayer that fits very nicely us also, I think some of you know it—so we will pray together. . . .

"Let us thank God for the opportunity that we all have together today for this gift of peace that reminds us that we have been created to live that peace and that Jesus became man to bring the good news to the poor.

"The news was peace to all of good will, and this is something that we all want—the peace of heart. Today the greatest means, the greatest destroyer of peace is abortion, and we who are standing here, our parents wanted us. Millions are dying deliberately by the will of the mother, and this is the greatest destroyer of peace today. Because if a mother can kill her own child what is left? For me to kill you and you to kill me. We are fighting abortion by adoption, and we have a tremendous demand for families who have no children. We are doing another thing which is very beautiful. We are teaching our people natural family planning. They practice this natural way by abstaining and self-control, by chastity, without destroying the life that God created in us.

"I think that we in our family, we don't need bombs or guns to destroy or to bring peace—just get together, love one another, bring that peace, that joy, that strength of presence of each other in the home and we will be able to overcome the evil that is in the world.

"Love begins at home, it is not how much we do, but how much love we put in the action that we do. To God Almighty how much we do does not matter, but how much love we put in that action. How much we do to Him in the person that we are serving. And let us all meet each other with a smile, for the smile is the beginning of love. Let us keep that joy of loving Jesus in our hearts and share the joy with all that we come in touch with. [And, then with a touch of holy irony] Just as I have said today, if I don't get to heaven for anything else, I will be going to heaven for all the publicity because it has purified me and sacrificed me and made me really ready to go to heaven."

She closed her address with these words: "I think that this is something; that we must live life beautifully. We have Jesus with us and he loves us. If we could only remember that God loves us, and we have an opportunity to love others as he loves us, not in big things but in small things with great love, then Norway becomes a nest of love. And how beautiful it will be that from here a center for peace from war has been given. If you become a burning light of peace in the world, then really the Nobel Peace Prize is a gift of the Norwegian people. God bless you."

And so Mother Teresa flew home from Norway bearing that gift of peace to her people, her beloved poor. It was something beautiful for God.

Brother Lazar returned to his home in Palermo where he has by now retired from the army; but Mother Teresa fights on for her King with her guided missiles of love. And should she be asked: "What will happen to your order when you 'go home,' Mother?" she would say: "God will decide."

Sources

Desmond Doig, *Mother Teresa: Her Work and Her People* (San Francisco: Harper and Row, 1980).

Malcolm Muggeridge, *Something Beautiful for God* (New York: Doubleday, 1977).

Robert Serrou, *Teresa of Calcutta: A Pictorial Biography* (New York: McGraw Hill Book Co., 1980).

Kathryn Spink, *Brotherhood of Man under the Fatherhood of God* (New Malden, England: Colour Library International Ltd., 1981).

Mother Teresa of Calcutta, *A Gift for God* (San Francisco: Harper and Row, 1974).

Courtesy of the Dohnavur Fellowship, London.

TWO

Amy Carmichael
of India

by Elisabeth Elliot

WHEN I WAS FOURTEEN years old, a student in boarding school, I first heard of Amy Carmichael. The headmistress of the school often quoted her writings and told of her amazing work in India for the rescue of little children in moral danger. No other single individual has had a more powerful influence on my own life and writing than Amy Carmichael. No one else put the missionary call more clearly.

Of the thirty-six books she wrote, I think it was the little book *If* that I read first, and found in it the source of an exhortation we heard often in the evening vespers services: Hold your friends to the highest. *If* is a series of statements about love, given to her sentence by sentence, Amy Carmichael claimed, "almost as if spoken aloud to the inward ear." Each page holds a single sentence, with the rest of the page blank. Someone has suggested that the blank space is for each of us to write in large letters GUILTY. I was seared by the words.

"If I fear to hold another to the highest because it is so much easier to avoid doing so, then I know nothing of Calvary love." I was guilty.

"If I can enjoy a joke at the expense of another, if I can in any way

23

slight another in conversation, or even in thought, then I know nothing of Calvary love." Such jokes, such slights were habitual with me.

"If I make much of anything appointed, magnify it secretly to myself or insidiously to others . . . then I know nothing of Calvary love." Every page pointed up my guilt, but every page aroused in me a deep longing to know that love, to be like the One who showed it to us on Calvary, and to follow him.

As a student in college I wrestled with the desperate desire to be married. I had promised the Lord I would go to some foreign land as a missionary, but I hoped I would not be required to go single. By this time I had memorized many of the poems in *Toward Jerusalem.* One of those that became my prayer then, articulating what my heart wanted to say but could not have found the words for was,

> Hold us in quiet through the age-long minute
> While Thou art silent and the wind is shrill:
> Can the boat sink while Thou, dear Lord, art in it?
> Can the heart faint that waiteth on Thy will?

There was a strong and practical everyday sort of faith that ran through all her writings, an immediate appropriation of the promises of God and an exquisite artistic sensitivity that drew me like a magnet. I read everything of hers that I could get my hands on, and soon my diaries were peppered with quotations labeled "AC."

She was born on December 16, 1867, in Millisle, Northern Ireland, of a Scottish Presbyterian flour miller named David Carmichael and his wife Catherine Jane Felson, a doctor's daughter. The eldest of seven children, she often led the rest of them in wild escapades, such as the time she suggested they all eat laburnum pods. She had been told that the pods were poisonous, and thought it would be fun to see how long it would take them to die. They were discovered, and a powerful emetic was administered in time to foil their plans for suicide. Once she led her little brothers up through a skylight onto the slate roof. They slid to the lead gutters and were walking gaily around the edge when they looked down to see their horrified parents staring up at them.

She was educated by governesses before she attended a Wesleyan Methodist boarding school in Harrogate, Yorkshire. It was there she saw that there was something more to do than merely "nestle" in the love of God, "something that may be called," she wrote later, "coming to Him, or opening the door to Him, or giving oneself to Him.... Afterwards, when I began to understand more of what all this meant, I found words which satisfied me. I do not know who wrote them:

> Upon a life I did not live,
> Upon a death I did not die,
> Another's life, Another's death,
> I stake my whole eternity."

When she was seventeen, seeing on the street in Belfast a poor woman in rags, carrying a heavy bundle, she had what amounted almost to a vision of the things that really matter in life. She and her two brothers, moved with pity for the poor soul, helped her along, though they were embarrassed to be seen with her. Amy described it as a horrid moment, for they were "not at all exalted Christians," but on they plodded through the gray drizzle. Suddenly words came to her, "Gold, silver, precious stones, wood, hay, stubble ... the fire shall try every man's work of what sort it is. If any man's work abide...." From that moment, for the rest of her life, it was eternal things that mattered.

She began children's meetings at home, then moved on to work at the Belfast City Mission, where she taught a boys' class and founded a group for the encouragement of Bible study and prayer called the Morning Watch. On Sunday mornings she taught a class for "shawlies," working girls who wore shawls because they could not afford hats.

One brother described her as "a wonderfully sincere, downright, unafraid, and sympathetic sister." Another said, "She was determined to get down to the root of things." Her sister's strongest impression of Amy concerned her enthusiasms. Nothing was impossible.

Her father died when she was eighteen, and the following year brought with it another moment of illumination. At a convention in Glasgow, when her soul seemed to be in a fog, she heard the words of the closing prayer, "O Lord, we know Thou art able to keep us from falling." It was as if a light shone for her. When her hostess took her to a restaurant for lunch and the mutton chop was not properly cooked, she remembered years later how trivial the chop was by comparison with those shining words, *able to keep us from falling.*

Her work with the shawlies grew so rapidly that a hall was soon needed that would seat five hundred people. The story of how that hall was paid for by one lady and how the land to put it on was given by the head of the biggest mill in the city is only the beginning of a lifetime of seeing a Heavenly Father's faithful provision for material needs as well as spiritual. She decided against receiving any money from those who were not utterly one with her aims, accepting it only when it was truly given to God. Amy Carmichael prayed for money and it came. She soon saw Bible classes, girls' meetings, mothers' meetings, sewing classes, and Gospel meetings being held in the hall which was called "The Welcome."

In 1888 all the family's money was lost, and they moved to England where Amy began another work for factory girls in Manchester.

It was on a snowy evening in January 1892 that a call which she could not escape and dared not resist came clearly: *Go ye.* A long and spiritually harrowing period followed as she sought to weigh her responsibilities to those who had never heard of Christ against responsibilities to her mother and, most agonizingly, to Mr. Robert Wilson, one of the founders of the Keswick Convention in England, to whom she had become like a beloved daughter. His wife and only daughter had died and Amy moved into the house. Although the situation was unusual, and not entirely to the liking of Wilson's two bachelor sons who also lived there, she believed it was God's place for her for a time. She loved and revered him, calling him "the D.O.M." (Dear Old Man) and "Fatherie" in letters to her mother. The thought of leaving him was a keen, sharp pain, something she had to lay on the altar, as it were, and trust God to take care of.

She thought of going to Ceylon, but then the knowledge that a million were dying every month without God in China prompted her to offer herself for that land. In July of 1892 she became the first missionary to be supported by the Keswick Convention, and went in September to the China Inland Mission headquarters in London. Geraldine Guinness, who later became the daughter-in-law of the mission's founder, Hudson Taylor, was one of those who encouraged and prayed for her there. She had purchased and packed her outfit when she received word that the doctor refused to pass her for service in China.

It must have been a blow, but did not in the least deter her in her purpose. She knew she had been called, and had no doubt that she would go—somewhere.

She sailed for Japan in 1893 to work under the Reverend Barclay F. Buxton of the Church Missionary Society and plunged into the work with joy, studying the language and adopting Japanese dress almost at once. It was there that she received a letter from her mother, asking whether she loved anybody very much. She gave an evasive answer. This is the only hint to be found anywhere that she might have had a chance to marry and perhaps was forced to choose between a man she loved and the call of God. Of course I am reading a great deal into the few words her biographer uses to cover this question, but because in my own experience it was such a burning one, I often longed to know more. I wished with all my heart that she had not been so everlastingly self-effacing and cautious in keeping herself out of her books.

Within a year, ill health took her to Shanghai, then to Ceylon, and a few months later she returned to England because the D.O.M. had had a stroke. His hopes were raised once more that she would remain with him.

During this time her first book was published, *From Sunrise Land*, a collection of letters she had written in Japan, illustrated with her own sketches. Again she received a medical rejection, and again she faced the unknown, still sure that the Lord who had called her so clearly would open a way somewhere, somehow. At last she was accepted by the Church of England Zenana Missionary Society at Keswick in July 1895 and arrived in Bangalore, India, in December with dengue fever and a temperature of 105. Some missionaries prophesied that she would not last six months. She lasted fifty-five years without a furlough.

Nearly a year later she met a missionary named Walker, who suggested that his district, Tinnevelly, was a much better place than Bangalore to learn Tamil, the language which the mission had assigned her to learn. Walker offered to be her teacher, and so it was in December 1896 that she reached the place which would be home for the rest of her life.

She was an excellent student. It was not that the language came easily to her. She prayed and trusted God for help, but she did what God could not do for her—she studied. She took comfort from the words of Numbers 22:28, "The Lord opened the mouth of the ass."

Amy lived with the Walkers in two different towns, where the number of Christians was pitifully small. She gathered together a band of Indian women to itinerate with her, among which was Ponnammal, who was to become an intimate, lifelong friend. They traveled at the rate of two or three miles an hour in a bullock bandy, a two-wheeled springless cart with a mat roof, "bang over stones and slabs of rock, down on one side, up on the other. Once we went smoothly down a bank and into a shallow swollen pool, and the water swished in at the lower end and floated our books out quietly" (*Things as They Are*, p. 5). They camped near the village at night, visiting in homes or wherever they could find women or children to talk to. Sometimes Walker and some of the men joined them for open-air meetings in the evening.

It was no lark. They found themselves in battle—the Lord's battle, to be sure, but one in which they were his warriors, up against a stupendous Force comprising principalities, powers, rulers of darkness, potentialities unknown and unimagined. She tried to describe it in a book called *Things as They Are*, but "How can we describe it?" she wrote. "What we have seen and tried to describe is only an indication of Something undescribed, and is as nothing in comparison with it." Nevertheless, even the understatement that she did put down on paper was rejected by publishers. It was much too discouraging. People wanted pleasanter stories, happier endings, so the manuscript was put in a drawer for several years until some English friends visited her, saw with their own eyes the truth of things, and begged her to allow them to try again to find a publisher willing to risk it. The book appeared in 1903. Its accuracy was questioned, so when a fourth edition was called for, letters were included from missionaries in India confirming in the strongest terms what she had written.

Amy had a clear eye and a keen ear. She wrote what she saw and heard, not what missionary magazines might have conditioned her to see and hear. One of them, for example, stated that Indian women think English women "fairer and more divine than anything imagined." But Amy heard them say when they saw her, "What an appalling spectacle! A great white man!" "Why no jewels? What relations? Where are they all? Why have you left them and come here? What does the government give you for coming here?"

"An old lady with fluffy white hair leaned forward and gazed at me with a beautiful, earnest gaze. She did not speak; she just listened and gazed, 'drinking it all in.' And then she raised a skeleton claw, grabbed her hair and pointed to mine. 'Are you a widow too,' she asked, 'that you have no oil on yours?' After a few such experiences that beautiful gaze loses its charm."

The notion of hungry "souls" eagerly thronging to hear the Gospel story is an appealing one and perhaps represents a true picture in some places but certainly not in South India, or, I found, in South America. I was very thankful for that book. *Things as They Are* told it to me straight, and thus prepared me for my own missionary work as few other books besides the Bible had done. It told of the great fortresses which are Hindu temples, and of the wickedness practiced there. It told of the utter indifference of most of the people when told of the love of Jesus. It told, too, of the few who wanted to hear.

"Tell me, what is the good of your Way? Will it fill the cavity within me?" one old woman asked, striking herself a resounding smack on the stomach. "Will it stock my paddy-pots or nourish my bulls or cause my palms to bear good juice? If it will not do all these good things, what is the use of it?"

It told of a boy who confessed Christ, an only son, heir to considerable property. He was tied up and flogged but he never wavered. At last he had to choose between his home and Christ. He chose Christ. The whole clan descended on the missionaries' bungalow, sat on the floor in a circle and pleaded. "A single pulse seemed to beat in the room, so tense was the tension, until he spoke out bravely. 'I will not go back,' he said." Though they promised him everything—houses, lands, a rich wife with many jewels—if only he would not break caste, though they told him how his mother neither ate nor slept but sat with hair undone, wailing the death-wail for her son, he would not go back. Later, Shining of Life (for that was his name) was baptized, and within a few weeks was dead of cholera. As he lay dying they taunted him. "This is your reward for breaking your caste!" "Do not trouble me," he answered, pointing upward. "This is the way by which I am going to Jesus."

During those first years, Amy Carmichael learned of the hideous traffic in little girls for temple prostitution. Calling them "the most defenceless of God's innocent little creatures" she gave herself to save them. She prayed for a way—she had not the least idea how it could be done, but she knew her Master, knew his limitless power, and believed him to show her.

She wrote letters (veiled, always, because the things she saw and heard were unprintable then) asking for prayer. She asked God to give her the words to say which would arouse Christians.

And thus God answered me: "Thou shalt have words,
But at this cost, that thou must first be burnt,
Burnt by red embers from a secret fire,
Scorched by fierce heats and withering winds that sweep
Through all thy being, carrying thee afar
From old delights. . . ."

In 1900 Amy went with the Walkers to camp in a quiet, out-of-the-way village called Dohnavur, and a year later the first temple child was brought to Amy, a girl of seven named Preena, whose hands had been branded with hot irons when she once attempted to escape. Gradually the child learned that she was to be "married to the god." She knew enough to detest the prospect and fled to a Christian woman who took her to Amy Carmichael. "When she saw me," Preena wrote fifty years later, "the first thing she did was to put me on her lap and kiss me. I thought, 'my mother used to put me on her lap and kiss me—who is this person who kisses me like my mother?' From that day she became my mother, body and soul."

And from that time on Amy Carmichael was called *Amma* (accent on the last syllable), the Tamil word for mother.

She began to uncover the facts of temple life. It was a system that had obtained from the ninth or tenth century. The girls trained for this service were sometimes given by their families, sometimes sold, usually between the ages of five and eight, but often when they were babies. They were certainly not "unwanted" children. They were very much wanted. In order to insure that they did not try to run away, they were shut up in back rooms, carefully watched, and, if they tried to escape, tortured as Preena was. They were trained in music and dancing, and, of course, introduced to the mysteries of the oldest profession in the world.

Amma's search for the children covered three years, but at last, one by one, they began to be brought to her. Soon it became necessary for her to have a settled place. Dohnavur, which she had thought of only as a campsite, proved to be the perfect answer. Indian women joined her, willing to do the humble, humdrum, relentless work of caring for children, work that they saw as truly spiritual work because it was done first of all for the love of Christ.

By 1906 there were fifteen babies, three nurses, and five convert girls training as nurses. There were no doctors or nurses to begin with, of course, not even any wet-nurses to help with the babies, since it was not the custom for village women to nurse a child other than their own. A number of babies died, some because they were frail when they arrived, some due to epidemics, some for lack of human milk. Amma grieved as any mother grieves, for they were her very own children. When one of the loveliest of them, a baby girl named Indraneela, died, Amma wrote,

Dear little hands, outstretched in eager welcome,
Dear little head, that close against me lay—
Father, to Thee I give my Indraneela,
Thou wilt take care of her until That Day.

In 1907 came the first gift of money to build a nursery. It was not long before Amma learned that boys, too, were being used for immoral purposes in the dramatic societies. Prayer began to go up for them, and by 1918 the work expanded to include them.

There were no salaried workers, either Indian or foreign, in the Dohnavur Fellowship. All gave themselves for love of the Lord, and no appeal was ever made for funds. When one sentence in a book she had written might have been construed as an appeal, Amma withdrew the book from circulation. No one was ever authorized to make pleas for money on their behalf. Needs were mentioned only to God, and God supplied them. The work grew until by 1950 or thereabouts the "Family" numbered over nine hundred people, including children and Indian and European workers. There was a hospital, many nurseries and bungalows for the children and their *accals* (sisters, as the Indian workers were called), a House of Prayer, classrooms, workrooms, storehouses, hostels, playing fields, fruit and vegetable gardens, farm and pasture lands. It was all "given." The financial policy has not changed to this day. The Unseen Leader is still in charge, and from him comes all that is needed from day to day, from hammocks in which the tiniest newborns swing, to modern equipment for the hospital. There are doctors, nurses, teachers, builders, engineers, farmers, craftsmen, cooks. There are none who are *only* preachers. A Hindu had once said to someone in the Dohnavur Fellowship, "We have heard the preaching, but *can you show us the life of your Lord Jesus?*" Each worker, whatever his practical task, seeks to show that life as he offers his service to his Lord.

The books *Nor Scrip, Tables in the Wilderness, Meal in a Barrel,* and *Windows* are records of God's constant provision for material needs, story after amazing story of his timing, his resources, his chosen instruments. The God who could provide food for a prophet through the instrumentality of ravens and a poor widow was trusted to meet the daily needs of children and those who cared for them, a few rupees here, a few thousand pounds there.

"An immense amount of rice is required for a family of nearly eight hundred," she wrote in 1943, "not counting guests and the poorest of the ill in the Place of Healing. Rice is brought from the fields unhusked. There has to be room for parboiling, drying, husking, and storing. Quantities of other things have to be stored; palmyra-palm sugar, coconuts, tamarind-pods, vegetables and fruit from our gardens, besides the spices which make curry what it is. And there are tins of oil, sacks of salt, shelves of soap. Then there are the miscellanea usually called sundries, such as lanterns, lamp-oil, rope, mats, extra cooking vessels, brass vessels, stocks of pots and pans, buckets and so on." (*Though the Mountains Shake,* p. 233)

"And He said to them, 'When I sent you out with no purse or bag or sandals, did you lack anything?' They said, 'Nothing.' " (Lk 22:35)

Amma was a woman of great reserve. Loving, unselfish, and outgoing to others, she was acutely aware of the dangers of drawing attention to herself in any way, or of drawing people to herself rather than to Christ. She could easily have become a cult figure, having great gifts of personality, leadership, and the ability to encourage the gifts of others. But she held strictly to Christ as Leader and Lord, and "coveted no place on earth but the dust at the foot of the Cross." In January 1919, her name appeared on the Royal Birthday Honours List. She wrote to Lord Pentland, "Would it be unpardonably rude to ask to be allowed not to have it? . . . I have done nothing to make it fitting, and cannot understand it at all. It troubles me to have an experience so different from His Who was despised and rejected—not kindly honoured." She was persuaded at last that she could not refuse it, but she did not go to Madras for the presentation ceremony.

There are a few pictures of her in the biography, but too few. I would love to have seen many more, but she refused to allow them to be taken, and although there are many pictures of the children and Indian workers in the books she wrote, none are included of herself or of other European workers.

Her biographer, Bishop Frank Houghton, tells us only that she was of medium height with brown eyes and brown hair. When I asked a member of the Fellowship to describe her she smiled. All she could think to say was, "She had wonderful eyes."

The light that seemed to shine in and through and around this woman was love. When asked what they remembered best about her, many people answered *love*. There is hardly a page of her books that does not speak of it in some way. Her poems are full of it.

Love through me, Love of God . . .
O love that faileth not, break forth,
And flood this world of Thine. (*Toward Jerusalem*, p. 11)

Pour through me now: I yield myself to Thee,
Love, blessed Love, do as Thou wilt with me. (p. 69)

O the Passion of Thy Loving,
O the Flame of Thy desire!
Melt my heart with Thy great loving,
Set me all aglow, afire. (p. 83)

When she thought her time on earth was nearly up she began to write letters to each one of the Family, which she put into a box to be opened after her death. These letters are steeped in love. One of them speaks of a misunderstanding that had arisen between two members of the Fellowship, and how deeply it had hurt her to hear of it. "Refuse it. Hate it," she wrote. "It may seem a trifle, but it is of hell. . . . If this were the last time I could speak to you I should say just these words, 'Beloved, let us love!' My children, our comrades in the War of the Lord, I say these words to you again, 'Beloved, let us love!' . . . We perish if we do not love."

The kind of love she lived and taught was no mere matter of feelings. It was steel. Though for many years she made it a practice to give each child a good-night kiss, she also believed in canings when canings were called for, but then she would wipe away the tears with her handkerchief. Sometimes she would pray with the child first, that the punishment might help her, and, after she had administered it, she found on at least one occasion that a glass of water effectively silenced the howls.

In her book about the spiritual training of an Indian nurse named Kohila she writes, "It was when she was given charge of a nursery with younger girls to train and to influence that the first difficulty appeared. . . . The alloy that was discovered in her gold was a weakness which leaned towards shielding a wrongdoer, or even sympathising with her, rather than taking the harder way of love without dissimulation, the noblest kind of help that soul can offer soul, and by far the most costly.

"Once, and this was indeed a grevious time, a special friend of Kohila's caused a younger one to stumble by teaching her to deceive. Kohila's judgment was influenced by her fondness for her friend. She admitted the wrongdoing but condoned it. . . . She forgot her Lord's solemn words about the millstone and the sea. Her sympathy was rather with the offender than with Him who was offended in the offence done to His little one.

"But syrupy affection never yet led to spiritual integrity. And though it looks so like the charity which is greater than faith and hope that it is 'admired of many,' it is not admirable. It is sin. And it is blinding sin." (*Kohila*, p. 75)

Again, in the little book *If:* "If I am afraid to speak the truth, lest I lose affection, or lest the one concerned should say, 'You do not understand,' or because I fear to lose my reputation for kindness; if I put my own good name before the other's highest good, then I know nothing of Calvary love" (p. 24).

One day in 1916 when the World War shadowed them with fear for the future, a group of seven Indian girls met with Amma to join themselves together as "The Sisters of the Common Life." They were young women who wanted to live a life of unreserved devotion, "a life without fences." They took their name from the Brotherhood of the Common Life, a religious community founded about 1380 in Holland by Gerhard Groot. They determined that there would be no line drawn between the spiritual and the secular, for Jesus drew no such line. Amma believed that the usual teaching about Mary and Martha was all wrong. It was not service that the Lord rebuked, but fuss. "The spirit can sit at the Master's feet while the hands are at work for others. Come unto Me and rest—take My yoke upon you."

If a job was to be done that nobody else wanted to do, someone would say, "Ask her. She is a Sister of the Common Life." They were ready to go to any lengths and to lay down their lives for others. They read books together in English, for the spiritual classics that had put iron into Amma's soul were not translated into Tamil. They were single women who believed it was God's will for them to remain single in order to serve him without distraction. Theirs was meant to be a life of joy, with nothing "dreary and doubtful" about it. It was a soldier's life. "The nearer the soldier is to the Captain the more he will be attacked by the enemy." (*Amy Carmichael of Dohnavur*, Frank Houghton, p. 219)

There were no vows in the technical sense. If any of them felt that God was giving them marriage, they could leave with no stigma attached to their leaving, but as long as they were in the group they acknowledged the Cross as the attraction. These were their rules:

My Vow: Whatsoever Thou sayest unto me, by Thy grace I will do it.
My Constraint: Thy love, O Christ my Lord.
My Confidence: Thou art able to keep that which I have committed unto Thee.
My Joy: To do Thy will, O God.
My Discipline: That which I would not choose, but which Thy love appoints.
My Prayer: Conform my will to Thine.
My Motto: Love to live: Live to love.
My Portion: The Lord is the portion of mine inheritance.

Teach us, good Lord, to serve Thee more faithfully; to give and not to count the cost; to fight and not to heed the wounds; to toil and not to seek for rest; to labor and not to ask for any reward, save that of knowing that we do Thy will, O Lord our God.

Amy Carmichael has been accused of opposing marriage as though it were God's "second best." It is a false accusation. She understood the power of the influence of a Christian home, and many of the children from Dohnavur as well as many of the workers have married. Some of these have continued as a part of the D.F. But she believed exactly what Paul believed, that those who do marry will have "trouble in the flesh," and cannot possibly be as free as the unmarried for certain tasks in the Lord's service. Many single women were needed to mother the hundreds of children. As boys were included, men were needed also, but the number of men who regarded celibacy as a divine call was small.

Amma was a woman peculiarly sensitive to beauty, as not only her writings but everything she touched will show. She was determined, as plans for each building were drawn up, that they should be beautiful. When they were planning the hospital, Dr. Murray Webb-Peploe asked if it might be too expensive. She hesitated to answer, but next day was June 4, for which the verse in the *Daily Light*, that marvelous little book of collected scriptures, was, "The house that is to be builded for the Lord must be exceeding magnifical." She took the word magnifical to mean "perfect for its purpose of glorifying the God of love, so that men and women will be drawn to Him. He is also the God of beauty, and it follows that ugliness jars. He has no pleasure in it—nor in dirt."

The long poems, *Pools* and *The Valley of Vision*, contain exquisite descriptions of the loveliness of the world around her, but delve deep into the mystery of its sorrow and suffering,

I saw a scarf of rainbow water-lace,
Blue-green, green-blue, lilac and violet.
Light, water, air, it trailed, a phantom thing,
An iridescence, vanishing as I gazed;
Like wings of dragonflies, a hint and gone—
Discovery was very near me then.
But no unseemly, no irreverent haste
Perplexes him who stands alone with God
In upland places. Presently I saw . . .

Father, who speakest to us by the way,
Now from a burning bush, now by a stream. . . .

Hers was a mystical mind. A true mystic is an utterly practical person, for he sees the Real as no pedant can ever see it, he finds the spiritual in the material (what T.S. Eliot calls "fear in a handful of dust," or Thomas Howard, "splendor in the ordinary"). George MacDonald said, "A mystical mind is one which, having perceived that the highest expression of which truth admits, lies in the symbolism of nature and the human customs that result from human necessities, prosecutes thought about truth so embodied by dealing with the symbols themselves after logical forms" (*Unspoken Sermons*).

She was logical. She was incisive, vigorous, utterly clear. She could write of a "scarf of rainbow water-lace," or she could use words that stab like a dagger or scorch like fire: "And we talked of the difference between the fleshly love and the spiritual; the two loves stood out in sharp distinction. In such an hour the fire of the love of God is searching. It knows just where to find the clay in us. That clay must be turned to crystal." (*Ploughed Under*, p. 187)

To a modern American it seems marvelous that a woman with what would seem to us little formal education and with no "degrees" should be able to use the English language so flawlessly, to shape a phrase so finely, and to write (very rapidly—sometimes twelve to fifteen hours a day) with such apparent ease and fluidity. There is not a word in any book or poem which Amy Carmichael had not bought by suffering. There is not an empty word, a superfluous word, a glib word. Every word, every line, has work to do.

In my recent rereading of the biography I found illumination of many passages which echo in my memory from her own writings. I found the circumstances which gave rise to those writings, the context in which she learned the lessons so lucidly set forth. Words given to her in the heat of battle have spoken strongly to me in the heat of my own experiences. They have been, in fact, the very voice of God to me, alive and powerful and sharp today as they were thirty or twenty-five or ten years ago.

There are markings, of course, in my copies of Amy Carmichael's books, as there are markings in every book on my shelves in which I have found real meat. The Amy Carmichael books in their uniform blue covers with lotus motif take up only half a shelf now, which makes me sad. Some of them have been "borrowed" and never found their way home. Others, to my great consternation, I left in a jungle house in Ecuador. Those I have are well-worn. Most bear the marks of mould and mildew and crickets, but they are my trusted friends. When I was in the throes of decision as to whether, newly widowed, I should take my small daughter and go to live with a remote tribe of Indians, I circled these words:

> His thoughts said, How can I know that it is the time to move?
> His Father said, And it shall be when thou shalt hear a sound of going in the tops of mulberry trees, that then thou shalt go out to battle. Thou shalt certainly hear that sound. [That sentence is underlined.] There will be a quiet sense of sureness and a sense of peace. (*His Thoughts Said*, 16)

I remember feeling doubtful about that "sound of going" in mulberry trees. There were no such trees in our jungle. Of course I knew that the words came from scripture (2 Sm 5:24 AV), but Amma had a disconcerting habit of quoting from many diverse sources, including the Bible, without citing the reference, and often without using quotation marks. It is flattering to the reader that she supposed us to be as well-read as she, and as spiritually advanced. I wasn't and I'm not, but I can testify to the Truth of what she wrote. The "sound of going" was different for her at different times, I'm sure, and the sign given to me in 1958 which led to my going to those Indians was not in any mulberry trees. But I found the promise fulfilled, "Thou shalt certainly hear that sound." God made it perfectly plain when the time came. I understood then her confidence, the sense of sureness and peace.

But subsequent decisions have put me in the same sort of quandary, and I have gone back again to the same little book.

> But the son still wondered what he should do if he did not
> hear a Voice directing him, till he came to understand that, as he
> waited, his Father would work and would so shape the events of
> common life that they would become indications of His will. He
> has shown also that they would be in accord with some word of
> Scripture which would be laid upon his heart. (19)

That made sense to me. No audible voices have ever told me what
to do, but the providential shaping of events and corroborating
scriptures given to me at the time have proved again and again the
trustworthiness of the Shepherd.

There have been one or two occasions when I have been falsely
accused by people on whom I had once had an influence for good. It
is a hard lesson to learn, and I am a slow disciple. There is a circle
around this one:

> Was He, whom he called Master and Lord, always understood?
> Was He never misjudged? They laid to His charge things that He
> knew not, to the great discomfiture of His spirit. Is it not enough
> for the disciple that he be as his Master and the servant as his
> Lord? (57)

Amma was visiting one day in 1931 in a nearby village where
there had been hostility to Christians. She fell into a pit which had
been dug "where no pit should be." The injuries did not heal, and
she suffered acute neuritis in her right arm, arthritis in her back,
chronic infections, and the cumulative effects of stress for the rest
of her life, hardly leaving her room until she died in January 1951 at
the age of eighty-three. During those twenty years as an invalid, in
nearly constant pain, she wrote fifteen books "out of the furnace,"
as it were, and the words of 2 Corinthians 1 show a part of the
service God gave her to do:

"Praise be to the God and Father of our Lord Jesus Christ, the
all-merciful Father, the God whose consolation never fails us! He
comforts us in all our troubles, so that we in turn may be able to
comfort others in any trouble of theirs and to share with them the
consolation we ourselves receive from God. As Christ's cup of

suffering overflows, and we suffer with him, so also through Christ our consolation overflows. If distress be our lot, it is the price we pay for your consolation, for your salvation." (2 Cor 1:3-6)

I am one of the many thousands, surely, for whose consolation and salvation Amy Carmichael paid a heavy price. That she paid it with gladness and a whole heart no one who has read even a page of hers could possibly doubt.

As I write these pages, my husband hands me a newspaper telling of the life of Henry Morrison Flagler, the American millionaire responsible for developing Palm Beach, Florida, as a playground for the very rich. In the early 1890s, the account states, he was looking for his life's "crowning challenge." It was, I remembered, a snowy night in 1892 when Amy Carmichael heard the call she could not escape and dared not resist: *Go ye.*

In 1894 Flagler built the Royal Poinciana, the world's largest resort hotel, accommodating two thousand. In that year Amy Carmichael was in Japan, where she wrote,

O for a passionate passion for souls,
O for a pity that yearns!
O for the love that loves unto death,
O for the fire that burns!

In 1896 Flagler opened his Palm Beach Inn, later to become The Breakers. That was the year in which Amma reached Tinnevelly, the part of South India where she would live out the rest of her life of service.

In 1901 Flagler's luxurious Whitehall, a marble palace built for his third wife, had been completed at the cost of four million dollars. In 1901 Preena, the first temple child, came to Amma, which meant the beginning of what would become the Dohnavur Fellowship.

"The Vanderbilts, Wanamakers, Astors, Goulds, Belmonts, and European royalty come to the magic island," the newspaper goes on, "awash in Caribbean splendor and Henry Morrison Flagler's grandeur."

"Gold, silver, precious stones, wood, hay, stubble . . . the fire shall try every man's work of what sort it is." These were the words that had come to Amy as a girl, when she stumbled along that Belfast street with the ragged old woman, words that defined for her forever the nature of man's choices. "If any man's work abide...he shall receive a reward." (1 Cor 3:14)

Like the mountaineer whose epitaph she loved to quote, she "died climbing." Now she is one of the great cloud of witnesses whose course has been finished, and who cheer us on to run the race that is set before us, looking as they did to Jesus, "who for the joy that was set before him, endured the Cross."

Sources

For information about the life of Amy Carmichael, I have relied on Frank Houghton's *Amy Carmichael of Dohnavur* (Fort Washington, Pennsylvania: Christian Literature Crusade, 1979) and on the following books by Amy Carmichael.

His Thoughts Said (Fort Washington, Pennsylvania: Christian Literature Crusade, 1949).

If (Grand Rapids, Michigan: Zondervan, 1968).

Kohila (London: SPCK, 1939).

Ploughed Under (Fort Washington, Pennsylvania: Christian Literature Crusade).

Things as They Are (Old Tappan, New Jersey: Revell, 1904).

Though the Mountains Shake (New York: Loizeaux Bros., 1946).

Toward Jerusalem (Fort Washington, Pennsylvania: Christian Literature Crusade).

Courtesy of Chosen Books.

THREE

Catherine Marshall

by Kathryn Koob

NOVEMBER 4, 1979—that day news reports raced across continents to reach a stunned American populace with the headline: "Americans Held Hostage in Iran. American Embassy Falls to Student Militants."

A diplomat in the American Foreign Service, my office was only two miles distant from the embassy. The report, phoned to me by an Iranian, was confirmed when I called the switchboard at the embassy in response to reports of student riots. *Embassy Occupied*— these words spoken by an Iranian voice at the end of the line confirmed the incredible truth. An international crisis of tremendous import was underway.

Along with some of the other members of my staff at the Iran-America Society, I spent the following thirty hours operating an ad hoc wire service to Washington, doing my best to keep the State Department abreast of developments reported on Iran radio and television. If we played our cards right, we could keep the lines of communication open for a few more hours before slipping off to safety. It seemed that the militants had forgotten about our office—at least for the present.

But by mid-afternoon November 5, all hope of safety was lost to us. The students came streaming into the building, and we were rounded up and taken by car through screaming mobs and into the American embassy compound.

Thus began 444 days of captivity. These days were not all filled with fear and hardship. Certainly, there was great fear, particularly in those first several hours, as well as hardship, but there was also consolation and blessing, the solace of knowing that God was God and that he cared. In the months that followed, he gave me numerous opportunities to recognize his faithfulness and to be thankful for his gifts, both great and small. Not the least of these was a book that came into my possession six months after I was taken captive—*The Helper* by Catherine Marshall. And what a helper it proved to be! Let me tell you about its author.

Catherine Marshall LeSourd has comforted, strengthened, and encouraged millions of people who have read her books. This woman, who as child was so shy that she hid whenever guests came to the manse to visit, acquired, as an adult, the rare gift of opening herself to the world, especially through her writing. In one of her most recent books she says, "Over the years a recurring theme in letters from the readers of my books has been, 'Dear Catherine: Forgive me for calling you by your first name, but through your books I feel I know you, that you are my friend'" (*Meeting God at Every Turn*, p. 15). Her joy has been that "the Spirit of God does reach down through the printed page . . . to speak to individuals in their own difficulties."

Born in Johnson City, Tennessee, she was christened Sarah Catherine, the first child of John Wood and Leonora Hazeltine Whitaker. Catherine's parents were far from wealthy, but they were rich in terms of their love for each other and for their three children, and they lived a full life as they moved from parish to parish in Tennessee, Mississippi, and West Viriginia.

Catherine describes her father as a scholar, a disciplined but loving individual who would dirty his fingers in coal dust to make his parishoners feel more comfortable shaking hands with him. His study was the center of their home wherever they lived, and it was always open to the children.

Her mother had a strong and steady influence on Catherine's life. In fact, she was the model for the heroine of Catherine's novel, *Christy*. It would be difficult to imagine anyone growing up under Leonora Wood's roof without adopting her attitudes toward marriage and family and her firm faith in God's goodness and love.

In *Meeting God at Every Turn*, Catherine entitled the chapter about her mother "Mother Never Thought We Were Poor." She compares her family's bounty to Mama's checking account in *I Remember Mama* by Kathryn Forbes. It was a nonexistent fund that kept the family going through many a crisis just because it was "there." Catherine describes her mother's account like this: "Suddenly in a blazing revelation it occurred to me that my own mother also had a bank account that kept us—her children—from being afraid. Her bank account too was real—as real as the mountain air we breathed and the nourishing bread she baked, as solid as the gold in Fort Knox. Mother's family bank account was her faith in the Lord, her absolute trust that the promise of give and it shall be given unto you' was as eternal as the mountains around us'" (*Meeting God at Every Turn*, p. 42).

When Catherine reached the age of seven, the Wood family grew with the arrival of a baby brother, Bob. Fourteen months later, a sister, Emmy, completed the family picture. Theirs was a "normal" family, deeply attached to one another, but not above the tensions, rebellions, anxieties, and problems that face all families. Inevitably the children played pranks and the parents lost their tempers and made an occasional unwise decision. But these momentary lapses were overshadowed by the strong, deep, mutual love that was expressed for one another and was a reflection of the love of Christ for each of his lambs.

Catherine's deep and abiding faith in the goodness of God—his ability to turn tragedy into promise—and his faithfulness began here, in this home. As a child she wondered at the source of her mother's strength and discovered that it was grounded in prayer. Determined that she, too, would know God's presence and love, Catherine asked her father if she could "join the church." She found that more was required than simply belonging to an organization; she must commit her whole life. When she gave it, she gave spontaneously and with deep conviction. Her future was in God's hands.

Encouraged to do her best at whatever she tried, Catherine decided to go to college. But it wasn't until she was accepted by the school of her choice, Agnes Scott College in Decatur, Georgia, that she realized there was not enough money to pay her tuition. Discouraged by this sudden insight, she threw herself across her bed, weeping tears of bitter regret. Her mother found her there and together they committed the problem to the Lord. Both parents decided that she should plan to go anyway. Almost miraculously, funds became available and Catherine went off to study.

During the years in Atlanta, she gave expression to a long-felt ambition to write. She steeped herself in literature and composition courses and began keeping a journal in earnest. "In it I would try to put down as accurately and memorably as I could my deepest feelings and reactions to life. A great earnestness about this had carried me through four years and several volumes." (*To Live Again*, p. 73)

While at Agnes Scott she met the pastor of Westminster Church—a popular young bachelor preacher. His name was Peter Marshall. The ensuing romance wasn't without its rough spots, at least from Catherine's point of view. On two different occasions she left Atlanta for summer vacation, determined to put the intriguing Peter Marshall out of her mind. But her efforts failed. Finally, during her senior year, he proposed to her and she accepted. They were married in November of 1936 and immediately moved to Peter's new parish in Washington, D.C.

It must have been a startling change for the young college graduate, barely out of her teens, to move from the campus of a fine women's school to the manse of one of the nation's most prestigious churches. But she did it graciously. She and Peter had committed their marriage to the Lord long before the ceremony ever took place. Determined to seek his will in their lives, they were sure that he would guide them in this venture.

Life in the manse was not unfamiliar to Catherine. She had lived in one all her life. But the duties incumbent on a minister's wife in the small southern congregations where she had grown up must have been far different than those in a large, metropolitan congregation. Yet, with the help of good friends, Peter's love for her, and her own background of love and good breeding, she bridged that chasm and the years of their Washington, D.C., ministry at New York Avenue Presbyterian Church were filled to overflowing.

Three years after their marriage, a son, Peter John, was born to them. By now Peter Marshall had become one of the nation's most influential ministers. He was the confidant of senators and congressmen and had been invited to become the chaplain of the United States Senate. He traveled across the country preaching and teaching. His presence at the New York Avenue church had resulted in expanded programs there. Life was full and busy.

Then, without warning, illness struck. The doctors could not diagnose Catherine's lung problem. Possibly tuberculosis. If so, it was not infectious, but it required total bed rest. This was a blow to Catherine, by now an active wife and mother. Yet she had no choice, and instead of the three or four months of immobility predicted by the doctor, she had to fight against the disease for almost two years.

Yet the time was not lost. She calls this period a time of "continuation in depth of the voyage of self-discovery and God-discovery begun in college" (*Meeting God at Every Turn*, p. 86). The most dramatic of these discoveries was the special power of the prayer of relinquishment. Catherine spent considerable time reading and studying what the Bible had to say about healing, and she prayed regularly to be healed. But her prayers seemed to go unanswered, and she became discouraged. Would she never again resume her activities as mother and wife? How could she face such a prospect?

In the midst of her discouragement she picked up the story of a missionary who had been ill for eight years. In a last, futile gesture, the missionary had given up everything to the Lord, including her wish to be well. This prayer of relinquishment inspired Catherine Marshall, and she prayed her own prayer: "I'm beaten, finished. God, You decide what You want for me." (*Adventures in Prayer*, p. 61)

The experience that followed is one that she relates in detail in

A Man Called Peter. Later that night she wakened. "Past all credible belief, suddenly, unaccountably, Christ was there, in Person, standing by the right side of my bed. I could see nothing but that deep, velvety blackness, but the bedroom was filled with an intensity of power, as if the Dynamo of the Universe was there. Every nerve in my body tingled with it, as with a shock of electricity. I knew that Jesus was smiling at me tenderly, lovingly, whimsically—a trifle amused at my too-intense seriousness about myself." (p. 168)

She was told to go and tell her mother about her experience, and she followed her Lord's command. The next step was to wait and see what the X-rays would reveal. Usually she awaited this test with anxiety. But not now. Perhaps she sensed that the healing process had begun. Her return to health was not instantaneous, but the X-rays indicated that real progress was being made against the disease. Slowly but surely Catherine Marshall was mending.

Prior to this extraordinary nighttime experience, she had been no stranger to the Lord and to his works and ways. Yet, this moment was so special that the memory of it must often have given her confidence and courage to strike out in new directions— to undertake the impossible and to rest secure in his wisdom during the storms of her lifetime.

The presence of God does not always seem as real as it did to Catherine Marshall that night, but the memory of that reality can give inspiration and courage long after the event.

This illness behind them, great things seemed in store for the Marshalls. But even as Catherine's own healing was underway, Peter was stricken with a heart attack. The taxing demands of a too-busy life were taking their toll. It was March of 1946 and the lessons learned in the prayer of relinquishment were needed once again. Catherine's was not the only prayer offered for her husband's life. People throughout the country prayed for Dr. Peter Marshall to recover, and he did.

Peter's doctors advised him to slow down if he wanted to live longer. But this was a difficult thing to ask of a man like Peter. As soon as he could, he was back at his schedule, working, traveling, and preaching as though he had never been ill.

Almost three years were to pass. Busy times, full of love, work, and play. The Marshall's spent pleasant summers at *Waverley*, their cottage on Cape Cod, where they could rest and relax and where Peter could work in his garden. Peter John was growing: a curious, vital, intelligent child. He and his father delighted in their time together, sharing in private nonsense games and sports.

Then, suddenly, this happy existence was shattered. Peter Marshall was stricken with another heart attack in January 1949. The sparkling eyes, the warm voice, the man dedicated to the will of God ceased to exist on this earth. Catherine was a widow, her son fatherless.

The fruit of Catherine's love for God and her search for his will in her life came to her aid. During the first days of her loss, she was sustained by an overwhelming sense of God's presence. Having lived her life so close to God, it is not surprising that the first thing she did when her husband was taken to the hospital was to pray. During this prayer, she experienced the "mother love" that God as Creator expresses for all his creatures. She was gathered into his arms and given the impression that all would be well. She describes it this way: "Suddenly the unexpected happened. Over the turbulent emotions there crept a strange all-pervading peace. And through and around me flowed love as I had never before experienced it. It was as if body and spirit were floating on a cloud, resting—as if Someone who loved me very much were wrapping me round and round with His love." (*To Live Again*, p. 27)

But all was not well. A few hours later, Peter Marshall went home to his Father. Even so, Catherine was sustained by the knowledge that her loving Father had not left her alone but was there with her—even in moments of deepest grief and anxiety.

Later, as she gazed on the still face, the shell of what was once the man she loved, she knew suddenly that the room was not empty. Again, her own words describe the sense: "I was not alone. For a while there was a transcendent glory. Though I did not understand it then and cannot explain it now, I knew Peter was near me. And beside him, another Presence, the Lord he had served through long years." (*To Live Again*, p. 14)

These experiences were to carry her through the days immediately following Peter's death. They gave her the inner strength and comfort necessary to make arrangements for the funeral service, to attend church services the first Sunday after that, and to meet the many people who demonstrated their love to the Marshall family at the time of this tragedy.

God was at her side. She knew he would be. But never had she expected such magnificent demonstrations of his love and strength. It must have been the knowledge of his care that helped her to quietly assess the assistance given her by the church board in sorting out her business affairs. With hard-headed practicality they pointed out the limited income available to her, the cost of maintaining a car, and the cost of dwelling space.

After the practicalities and good wishes had come to an end and the door closed behind these men, Catherine started thinking again. Perhaps her mind returned to that time years ago when a college education seemed impossibly out of reach. She would remember her mother's straightforward solution to that problem. God's will would be done.

It can't have been easy for the young widow to have sorted out her life and started over. And this certainly was complicated by the fact that Dr. Marshall had been so well-known and a bit of him claimed by so many people. Yet, from many sources a single idea began to evolve.

Peter Marshall had refused to have his sermons printed in book form during his lifetime. He had often been asked for reprints, and these requests did not stop with his death. Was there sufficient interest to warrant the publication of a book? The answer was yes, and Catherine set out, with the aid of many friends, to begin the complicated task of sorting, selecting, and editing the sermons for publication.

Mr. Jones, Meet the Master was the result, and it sold out rapidly. It is still in print, and still offering words of inspiration, encouragement, and hope to thousands of readers. Catherine wrote the introduction. Here was an opportunity to talk about the spirit of the man who had been her husband. Her years of journal-keeping and her long interest in writing stood her in good stead for the task. This brief introduction represented the beginning of an entirely new ministry for her.

Through the swirl of autograph parties, best-seller lists, and thousands of letters from those who responded to the book, Catherine still had to deal with the very real problems of finding a place to live, of caring for her son, and coping with life as a single person. The extraordinary popularity of *Mr. Jones, Meet the Master* led to a request for a second volume.

After careful thought, Catherine proposed, instead, a biography of her famous husband. This venture took a tremendous amount of time and emotional energy, yet it filled her days with remembered love. The result was *A Man Called Peter.*

As Catherine began writing the story she had lived, she evaluated her desire to write. She had always felt compelled to put her thoughts on paper and writing had become as essential as breathing. During her life she had struggled with the question of why she wanted to be a writer. She wanted to write for the good of others, to make a contribution of lasting value.

Now she had the chance to tell Peter's story. A book about a wonderful man. But more than that, it would be the story of one of God's servants. A book that would be written to God's glory. Her aim was to use the "life of this one man then, this fallible man, Peter Marshall, . . . to answer the average person's questions about God and how He deals with each of us." (*To Live Again*, p. 139)

Catherine Marshall has never deviated from this decision in any of the books she has written. For this reason, more than any other, they speak to the ordinary individual. The problems she talks about are real. The people in her books have personalities and feelings, and they are just like one's own family. Her commitment to God and his will is simple, direct, and personal. There is room for human error and she opens herself wide to observation—exposing her faults, foibles, and successes.

A Man Called Peter was a resounding success. Close to the top of the *New York Times* best-seller list for a year and a half, it reached the hearts and minds not only of those who knew him, but of countless thousands of others. God was at work in a marvelous way. One of the greatest surprises was that the book appealed to so many teenagers.

I was one of them. I have always loved books, reading anything that came to hand. My mother bought a copy and the entire family read it, cried over it, and were inspired by it. I remember thinking that it was a beautiful story written about a servant of God by another of his servants. In the early years of the 1950s ecumenism was not a word that was known widely in church circles, at least not in Jubilee, Iowa, where I grew up, but here was a book that transcended denominational lines and spoke to the matter of servanthood. And besides, it was a good story. We were proud that a Christian book could be a best-seller.

This was my first encounter with Catherine Marshall. She didn't enter my life again for many years. Occasionally I would see magazine articles written by her, always lovely to read, but so were a lot of other things. I can almost see her smile at this point, and I can hear her say softly, "But in God's own time. . . ."

What was Catherine's life like after she published her second book? She was a celebrity with two best-sellers to her credit, though she insisted that *Mr. Jones, Meet the Master* was really Peter's. There was talk of a film and incessant demands were made on her for autograph parties, tours, and public appearances. She tried to answer personally the letters that came her way. So many of them were filled with wonderful insights, sharing the innermost secrets of the writers.

Though she had become a celebrity, she was still a young widow, learning to cope with grief. Dealing with the problems of being a single parent were an everyday event. Her books *To Live Again* and *Beyond Ourselves* are filled with vignettes from her life during those lonely years and with stories of how she sought to deal with those problems. Most striking is her constant willingness to "go to the one place I could count on for final authoritative truth—the Bible." She disciplined herself daily, whether writing, researching, or establishing a special quiet time for study, prayer, and meditation.

Catherine had an incredible capacity for growth and was not

afraid to admit her shortcomings. She knew firsthand the tempta-
tion and weakness that challenge all of us and related these freely
in her books.

When asked about her candor and willingness to share many of
the details of her private life, she put her answer squarely in the
context of God's will. "It is important," she says, "that we should be
utterly frank with ourselves in establishing a relationship with
Jesus Christ. It is the only way to establish a true relationship with
him. This frees us to confess our shortcomings, and it is this
freedom which helps us realize that we are very important spirits
living in this body here on earth. Then we can make connections.
It's only then that we find the spirit of the other person and share at
that level. That's when we find this kind of candor. This is truly the
communion of saints."

Loneliness is something we all must deal with and Catherine
Marshall had to deal with it—as a celebrity. Being in the public eye
is often much lonelier than you might think. Someone is almost
always looking over your shoulder with the result that you are
haunted by a horrible feeling that if you slip into a peevish tone of
voice, or even worse, have a temper tantrum, the whole incident
will be blown out of proportion.

And then there are the times when you sit alone because people
are sure you have so many invitations that theirs would be an
imposition. All of this is compounded by the self-imposed
loneliness that occurs when you cannot bring yourself to shake
one more hand or smile sweetly for one more minute.

Catherine had experienced a loving and fruitful marriage. She
was human, and she longed for the companionship of a husband. In
seeking God's will, she put herself in his hands. She says, "I stopped
thinking about remarriage. Not that the desire was wiped out, just
that it had become much less important to me. My perspective had
changed. This was the Lord's doing, of course, and came about
because I was able to give the matter over to Him to handle."
(*Meeting God at Every Turn*, p. 172)

In 1959 Catherine Marshall married Leonard LeSourd, then the
Executive Editor of *Guideposts* magazine, and thus began another

chapter in her life. The frustrations and joys of life with the LeSourd family led her to plumb even more deeply the strength and wisdom of the Lord.

While all this was happening in her life, my own life was developing, sometimes along parallel lines. I, too, was dealing with the problem of loneliness and seeking patience and the wisdom of God for my life's direction. My learning and growth had not been as disciplined as Catherine's, but I had learned certain lessons in my travels.

God had been good. My life was full and rich. He had blessed my career beyond my wildest childhood ambitions. I was no longer the speech and drama teacher I had dreamed of becoming as a third-grader, but a diplomat in the Foreign Service of my country.

My job had taken me to many places. I was traveling and meeting people—all kinds, including missionaries who had given their lives to the work of the Lord in remote, underdeveloped areas. I had talked with people who served God under repressive governments. My own country's freedoms, particularly of speech and worship, had taken on new significance for me.

The interludes when I was in the States on assignment and could be in contact with my own church were increasingly precious as I met with Bible study groups, taught Sunday School, and gathered strength for the next long dry spell away from my own religious community.

In 1979, knowing that my next assignment was to a country that was 95 percent Muslim, I studied a bit about Islam and poured over the Old Testament history books to see how many biblical sites I might actually be able to visit. Little did I know that on this trip to Iran I would never see the place where Esther, that courageous Jewish woman, had lived. Instead, amid the clamor of militant Iranian crowds, I would encounter another courageous woman, Catherine Marshall!

My first day of captivity was November 5, 1979. Only one other woman was held for the full 444 days. Her name was Elizabeth Ann Swift (Ann), and she became my roommate in March of 1980. Shortly after that, sometime after Easter, we were taken to a room in the embassy which had been established as a "library." The sections were labeled fiction, biography, science fiction, sports, and religion.

We stood there for a moment, our blindfolds in our hands, looking in awe at the books. Up to that time we had had less than a choice selection brought around to our rooms in a grocery cart. From that cart I had selected and read such fascinating works as *Scuba Diving in Caves*, *The 1976 Football Yearbook*, and *A History of Bell Telephone*. Here was wealth! We looked the titles over, carefully selecting some old favorites and some new authors, too.

I moved to the religion shelf. What would be there? Just a few weeks earlier we had been given some books sent by a friend of mine: *Clap Your Hands!* by Larry Tomczak, *God Did Not Ordain Silence*, and a concordance of New Testament scripture passages relating to the Holy Spirit. All three books had been filled with the fruits of the Spirit and had been so important to us as we studied them during Holy Week. Would there be something on the shelf that would carry on our study?

"Ann, look," I said. "Thomas à Kempis' *Imitation of Christ*. Shall I take it?" She nodded and I slipped it onto the stack of books in my arms.

"This looks like a new book," I said pulling another slim volume off the shelf. "Catherine Marshall . . . might be good." I opened the cover and there, printed at the top of the page and leaping out at me were the words, "Love from your niece, Emma Louise."

I could hardly contain my joy—or my anger! This was *my* book from my ten-year-old niece and *they* hadn't given it to me!

When we got back to the room, I filled Ann in on what happened. I still didn't realize what the subject of this little volume called *The Helper* was.

My joy at finally receiving this gift from Emma Lou overcame my anger at the students, and I placed the book with my Bible to await next morning's study time. That night my prayers included a "thank you" for the book.

The next morning I opened *The Helper* and read the foreword. I discovered that it was about the Third Person of the Trinity—the Comforter on whose presence I had been relying so heavily since the first day of my captivity. The Giver of heavenly gifts, the Spirit who guides and leads our lives was the subject of this book.

I had experienced his manifestation in so many ways, and here was a systematic look at him, telling who he is and how he helps us. I was quite sure Catherine Marshall would not get carried away in an ecstasy of emotion. Anyone who had come from her background wouldn't. And in her foreword she had explained the deliberate method of study she had used to prepare this manuscript. Besides, she and Peter Marshall had initiated this study together.

My dilemma was whether to read slowly and savor, or to give in to the urge to take in as much of it as I could, as quickly as possible. I compromised. Never more than two short chapters at a time, but I could (and did) go back more than once a day. By now I had read the New Testament several times and the Old Testament in its entirety at least once, and some parts many times. I welcomed the guide this study would give me. I really wanted to find out how this woman, so much in the public eye, had dealt with a subject that was so sensitive to some people, particularly in the so-called conservative mainline denominations.

I knew from my own experience the wonderful presence of God in moments of severe stress, and I was anxious to see what I would find. I could understand the concept of God the Creator, Father and Giver of Life. And Jesus had been part of my life since I was very young. Since the day after my capture, the Holy Spirit's presence had been a constant source of comfort—yet there was something so mysterious and frightening to me about the Spirit, especially about his gifts. I knew that the gifts of healing and tongues had torn congregations and families apart.

Still, from catechetical instruction, I understood that my own faith was the work of the Holy Spirit. How often had I said those words of Dr. Martin Luther's, explaining the Third Article of the Creed, Sanctification:

I believe that I cannot by my own reason or strength believe in Jesus Christ my Lord or come to Him, but the Holy Ghost has called me through the Gospel, enlightened me with His gifts and sanctified and preserved me in the true faith. . . .

But this did not spell out those gifts which Paul talks about so clearly in Galatians 5:22: "But the fruit of the Spirit is love, joy, peace, patience [did I need that one!]." And again in 1 Corinthians 12:8-10, Paul says ". . . to another gifts of healing by that one Spirit, to another miraculous powers, to another prophecy. . . ."

What would I find in *The Helper?* I started reading eagerly. In the summer of 1944, Catherine Marshall was led to do an exhaustive study of the Holy Spirit. Aware of the limited materials available on this subject, she made what I have come to regard as one of her trademark decisions. She tells about it in the foreword of the book:

"I decided to go to the one place I could count on for final authoritative truth—the Bible. Scripture had never yet deceived me or led me astray. From long experience I knew that the well-worn words from an old church ordinance had it exactly right—the Bible still is 'the only infallible rule of faith and practice.'

"At the same time I also knew that the search in Scripture could be no random dipping in; it had to be thorough and all inclusive. A Bible, a Cruden's concordance, a loose-leaf notebook, pen and colored pencils were my only tools." (pp. 11-12)

One chapter particularly made an impression. It was called "He Is My Remembrancer." The biblical basis for this concept is John 14:26: "But the Counselor, the Holy Spirit, whom the Father will send in my name, will teach you all things and *will remind* you of everything I have said to you." (Italics mine.)

I had already experienced a multitude of these remembrances as I filled my days by searching my mind for the scripture verses and hymns I had learned as a child. Here was Catherine Marshall encouraging me to lean more heavily on this gift, and I did. Bits and pieces of the catechism learned years before floated into place and notes from college Bible classes seemed to rise up to challenge my thinking. I have continued to rely on this help even since my return as I plow through piles of accumulated letters, clippings, and notes.

One of the most important passages for me during this time was Luke 21:12, 14-15: "And you will be brought before kings and governors and all on account of my name. . . . But make up your mind not to worry beforehand how you will defend yourselves. For I will give you words and wisdom that none of your adversaries will be able to resist or contradict."

It was easy to borrow trouble by wondering what questions the student militants would ask next. Could this passage have bearing on my own situation? The students weren't kings, but they were in power. I wasn't being held because I was a Christian, but I knew that this promise was for me here and now.

Reading *The Helper* reaffirmed my own thoughts and actions. Here was written witness to the strength, power, and variety of the Holy Spirit's ministry in many lives, and particularly from one who had experienced many trials and still looked to God for comfort and direction.

From then on it was a treasure hunt each time we went to the library. Would we find another book by Catherine Marshall? We did. *Something More, To Live Again, Beyond Ourselves*—all sent by "friends" of hers. They paid her the greatest compliment they could, sending us their well-worn, underlined, and annotated books. We also found *Christy* and kept looking for more.

Reading about Catherine Marshall's methodical habits of study and record-keeping, of maintaining prayer diaries and lists, encouraged me to keep a spiritual diary during the latter part of my captivity. In it I recorded my feelings and struggles, and I have come to consider this spiritual "note-taking" an important part of my spiritual life even now. I am not as faithful as I was in Iran, but I know the value of writing down my thoughts, my questions, and God's answers.

In the book *Something More* I found the prayer that has helped many Christians in dangerous and troublesome spots. Here was a prayer that was so short, so simple, that I could carry it in my head. It was really an affirmation of faith.

The Light of God surrounds me.
The Love of God enfolds me.
The Power of God protects me.
The Presence of God watches over me.
Wherever I am, God is.

I repeated this affirmation/prayer of faith as a litany each day during my exercise period. I would think of the blessings that had been bestowed on me during this time—of how God had protected his saints through the ages and surrounded them even in death with his presence. This prayer was a wonderful gift.

During my captivity, I was faced with a major challenge—to obey the Lord's command to love my enemies. This was perhaps the most difficult lesson I had to cope with in my captivity. Catherine Marshall offered insight and wisdom here, too. She reminded me that God's forgiveness to man is related to man's forgiveness to his fellow man. As my experience in Iran recedes, this lesson stands out, and it is one that grows in magnitude with each passing day. As Catherine Marshall points out, the need is not only for one person to forgive another, it is for nations and peoples to look to each other with compassion and forgiveness rather than with envy, hatred, and a longing for revenge.

Catherine's ability to open her life to so many has certainly been a model for me since my return. How I have longed to turn my back on requests for a speech or "just one more question," until I remember how she has turned many private and personal events to public witness and gave of her life so that God might instruct and teach others.

Her ability to see God in action in the ordinary events of everyday life, and to relate this in a simple, direct fashion understandable to anyone who seeks guidance is a great gift. She has been a good steward of her talents. When I am distraught because I have too much to do, or I think I would like to escape to a community retreat for meditation and study, I am reminded by this woman that as Christ's followers we are in this world. When Christ came he did not establish a retreat center—though he sought a place apart regularly—but he moved and worked among the people of his time. Like the One she loves, Catherine Marshall works among the people of her time and place.

She says she could receive no greater compliment than being thought of as a friend because of her writings. But I think there is something more important than that. I am sure that the greatest compliment one could pay Catherine Marshall is to say, "Through you I saw God a little bit clearer." For that is her life's mission, and it was to his glory that her work has begun, and it is in his name that it will be completed. ›

Thank you, Catherine, for helping me to see God more clearly.

† † †

I was in Washington, D.C., when the first reports of Catherine Marshall's death reached me. What a sense of loss, and of regret. I had hoped to meet her for the first time this coming summer. Now that hope had dissolved in an instant. "But wait a minute," I could almost hear Catherine saying. "Aren't you forgetting that we're bound to meet—in glory? And what a meeting that will be, when neither of us need worry about any shortcoming, any earthly limitation!"

Yes, I reminded myself, my meeting with Catherine Marshall had only been postponed, not canceled. I laughed at myself for thinking anything else, and as I laughed I knew that it would be a meeting worth waiting for.

Sources

Adventures in Prayer (Lincoln, Virginia: Chosen Books, 1975).

The Helper (Lincoln, Virginia: Chosen Books, 1978).

Meeting God at Every Turn (Lincoln, Virginia: Chosen Books, 1980).

To Live Again (Lincoln, Virginia: Chosen Books, 1957).

FOUR

Adrienne de Lafayette

by Elizabeth Sherrill

I N 1794, IN PARIS, the French Revolution entered on its second
phase. The makeshift prisons remained crowded, but their
population changed: instead of former nobles, they now housed
petty thieves, looters, and black-market profiteers, as the revolutionary government instituted basic reforms.

In one of the mansions-turned-prison, however, lived an exception. Everything about this prisoner—the way she walked, ate,
spoke—marked her as a noblewoman. And the greatest difference
between her and her fellow inmates was not even visible: a small
silver crucifix pinned out of sight beneath her dress.

Here is the story I imagine her telling . . .

✝   ✝   ✝

The crowd outside the dining room was already beginning to
shove, though the door would not be opened for an hour. Usually I
stayed out of it, waiting in my garret room on the fifth floor until
the drum for the single meal of the day sounded. It didn't take a
great deal of food, after all, to keep me alive.

Today, though, I struggled to keep my place near the door. Today

I must get to the bread tray before it is empty.

Verminous bodies pressed against me until I could scarcely breathe. If only I were taller, big enough to shove back! It was only since I'd been a prisoner that I had been aware of my size. I'd known, of course, that my husband stood far, far above me, but that was because he was extraordinarily tall, at six-feet-three-inches always the tallest man in any room, stooping a bit as though trying to get in touch with the rest of the world.

Gilbert . . . my love . . . are you still alive!

With the press of people jostling, suffocating, I closed my eyes and saw my husband looking down at me. The long, narrow nose, the high, sloping forehead, the powder from his wig drifting in a gentle snowfall onto the epaulets of his uniform. On tiptoe I would stretch up to brush them off. And he would smile that shy awkward smile: "Where did I ever find such a tiny wife?"

In those days it was a joke. When had I ever needed to reach for anything? As long as I could remember there had been footmen to place my food in front of me, pages to run my errands. Only in these last two terrible years had I learned that those with the longest legs got to the table first, those with the longest arms filled their soup bowls.

"Hi! Look who's here!"

With a sinking heart I knew that I had been spotted. Other voices took up the cry, gleefully passing on the news: "The great lady is dining with the serfs today!"

"What an honor!"

"She'll soil her satin gown"—a woman's voice—"rubbing shoulders with us riffraff!"

How long had it been, I wondered, since I had worn satin? The only clothes I owned were this rumpled linen dress and this torn woolen shawl, no match for the midwinter cold.

At last, the rat-tat-tat of the drum! The double doors swung inward; the crowd surged forward. Running, stumbling, I struggled toward the wooden bread-trencher.

"Look! The noble lady can scrap for her supper like any fishwife!" A wooden shoe came down painfully on my instep. It didn't matter.

My hand had closed around a chunk of coarse black bread.

From the rear door the pot of barley gruel was carried in and the crowd turned in that direction. I would not even try for a bowlful today: I would eat some of the bread. After all, it wasn't a very big piece that I needed for . . . tonight.

Tenderly I broke off a portion and tucked it into the sash of my dress. Then I found a place on one of the benches ringing the walls and began to gnaw on my prize.

This must have been a charming room once, I thought, gazing up at the painted ceiling. High above the wine-spattered floor the god Apollo still pursued the nymph Daphne across a forest glade. That hook in the very center had doubtless held a crystal chandelier, and there would have been vases on that green marble mantel. All gone now, of course, and the house turned into a prison, as so many great homes in Paris had been since the Revolution.

Somehow the unused fireplace made the room colder still. I thought of our own home, Gilbert's and mine, only four streets away, where at this time of year, December, there were always fires crackling on every hearth. Not December, I corrected myself, looking around guiltily. There was no month of December. This was the month of Frimaire, in the year three of the new world of Liberty, Equality, and Fraternity.

I swallowed another mouthful of the bitter black bread. For months the bakers had been mixing plaster with flour to increase the weight of their loaves, but this bread was maggoty as well.

The hollow-cheeked old woman beside me on the bench seemed to read my thoughts. "Criminals, that's what these bakers are, Citizeness! Not that I could chew it anyway—not if it was cake baked by Marie Antoinette herself!" She opened her mouth to reveal toothless gums and a winey breath.

I swallowed again, willing my stomach not to revolt. *You may be alive, Gilbert! You must be alive! And therefore I too want to live.* My companion hobbled off to join the group around the wine jar. I forced down the last of the bread and followed her. That was the other thing I needed for this night of nights, a little wine—though in this case the problem would not be getting it, but carrying it unnoticed up to my room. Bread and soup disappeared as soon as they arrived, but there was a seemingly inexhaustible supply of thin vinegary red wine.

I took a wooden bowl from the table and wiped the greasy rim as unobtrusively as I could. My concern for cleanliness had often brought hoots from my fellow prisoners.

"May I have some wine, Citizen?" I asked the sullen-faced trusty who occupied a three-legged stool beside the big wine jar.

He appeared not to see me.

"May I have wine, please?"

The man aimed a stream of tobacco juice at the green marble fireplace.

"Some wine, please, Citizen," I repeated hopelessly.

"*Please* will get you nowhere with the likes of him!" It was the old woman from the bench. "Out of the way, you lazy ox! If you won't do your job, I'll do it for you!"

She refilled her own bowl, then mine. And now . . . how to get it up to my room unseen! The daily meal was over; until the doors opened at this time tomorrow there would be nothing more to eat. But people lingered in the room, drawing at least an illusion of warmth from the nearness of other bodies.

A trusty was collecting wooden bowls from tables and benches; I thrust mine out of sight beneath my shawl. Another duty-prisoner began herding people toward the door. "Closing! Closing! Time to clean up!"

"Aye! There's time to clean up!" my toothless friend called back. "There's all the time in the world! Why don't you do it, then, to earn the rations you steal from the rest of us?"

"Out you go, granny," said the man, not unkindly. Besides being the oldest prisoner in the Maison Delmas she was a general favorite, a washerwoman who had stripped clothes from the headless victims of the guillotine to sell on the black market.

I edged with the others out the door, trying to keep my bowl with its precious contents from being bumped. Out in the vestibule people were settling down for the long, dull afternoon, reluctant to return to the icy rooms on the upper floors. I inched toward the stairs. Card players had settled on the bottom steps. But I must get past them to reach my room before Pere Carrichon arrived! For he would come, tonight, as soon as it grew dark enough to walk in the streets. If everyone else in Paris had forgotten what night this was, Pere Carrichon would remember.

At the foot of the broad, curved staircase I gathered my skirt into my free hand. "Pardon me, Citizens. May I disturb your game long enough to pass?"

"Her ladyship desires to pass, Emil!"

"On your knees, serfs!"

Would they never tire of the same stale jokes? Or of rushing to the foot of the stairs each time a woman started up? There were only a handful of us female prisoners in the Maison Delmas—mostly small shopkeepers convicted of hoarding—and the others handled the leering men with jeers of their own. Even the old washerwoman was more than a match for them, lifting her skirt around her bony knees and lamenting that there was not a man there who could inspire her to lift it any farther.

I alone was unable to control the tears that all my life had betrayed my feelings. Cheeks burning, I stepped over the sprawling figure of one of the card players and started the endless, circling climb. Usually I held my skirt tight against my side, but with the bowl held beneath my shawl, the other hand clutching the railing, I could only scramble up the stairs as fast as my legs would carry me, to the shrieks of merriment below.

The second landing. I circled the stairwell and groped up the third flight, hot tears blinding me. American women wouldn't cry, I thought suddenly, unexpectedly. They never cried, Gilbert said. The fourth landing. One more flight. This final stairway was narrow and steep, without a handrail. *Oh Gilbert! If I had been that kind of woman, would you have loved me more?*

The fifth floor at last. Mere cubicles of rooms up here. I hurried to the fourth one on the right and closed the door gratefully behind me. The glass was broken in the tiny dormer window and street noises from the Rue Notre Dame des Champs rose clearly: carts bumping over the pavement, the shouts of drivers. I set the wooden bowl tenderly on the chair that was the room's one piece of furniture, then knelt and groped in a corner for two stumps of candles I had hoarded there.

Already, at three o'clock this winter afternoon, it was growing dark. Here was the little pile of papers and quills with which I wrote every day, all day, to anyone who might know where my husband was. Not enough light for another letter today.

I found the candle ends and the tinderbox and stood up. Then, removing my shawl, I lifted the bowl of wine and spread the shawl over the seat of the chair. I put the bowl down again, precisely in the center, then took the piece of bread from my sash and placed it in front of the bowl. A candle on either side, the tinderbox on the floor close at hand.

One thing more. I unpinned from its hiding place beneath my bodice the silver crucifix Mamma had given on the day of my marriage. Gently I propped it against the chairback, feeling rather than seeing in the growing gloom, the figure of the Lord Jesus stretched upon the cross. It was far too small, of course, but a chair covered with a shawl was hardly a proper communion table, either. It was all I had, and Pere Carrichon, traveling the streets every day, liable to be stopped and searched at any corner, could carry nothing except what any carpenter might have in his tool bag.

A freezing rain drummed on the roof. I picked up the tattered blanket from the straw-filled sleeping pallet and wrapped it around my shoulders in place of the shawl.

And now that everything was ready I was seized with terror that Pere Carrichon would not come. What if he had been arrested . . . deported to the Indies! Surely in all this time someone would have reported him as a priest who had refused to take the oath of first-loyalty to the state. And even if he was free, he could be sick—starving. It wasn't only in the prisons that people were hungry: they said half of Paris was begging for bread this terrible winter.

Or . . . what if the guard downstairs at the door was not deceived by his carpenter disguise? Or suppose he had simply forgotten? No! Of that at least I was certain. He had not forgotten! If he was alive and if he was not in prison, he would try to come to me tonight. The rest of Paris might have forgotten. To the rest of France it might be only the thirteenth of Frimaire, year three of the Republic. To the two of us it was Christmas Eve in the year of our Lord 1794.

The chill rain gusted through the broken window. I crawled onto the straw and tucked my legs beneath me. What was the warmest thing I could think of? A blazing fire—Yes! Both dining-room fires crackling and glowing, on Christmas Eve in the Rue Bourbon. Just four streets away ...

There would have been Americans at our table, of course. Americans were always homesick at Christmas and so we invited all who were in the city. Monsieur and Madame John Adams. Monsieur Thomas Jefferson. Monsieur Gouveneur Morris. I smiled, remembering how shocked our servants had been, one year, when Monsieur Benjamin Franklin appeared at the table without a wig, and no decorations on his dinner jacket.

And after dinner, *four* fires lighted in the long ballroom. And in the midst of the dancing, my excuses to our guests as I left for midnight Mass. The gentlemen bending low over my hand, Gilbert's half indulgent, half apologetic explanation:

"My wife finds comfort in the ancient customs."

Smiles behind the ladies' fans. Was it possible that an educated person took church seriously enough to leave in the middle of a party? My coach waiting in the courtyard, footmen leaping up behind, the swift ride through the dark streets.

A wagon rattled past in the Rue Notre Dame des Champs five floors below. I leaned against the attic wall, imagining I was on my way to church. This threadbare blanket was a bearskin rug; on my lap was the sack of coins for the poor who crowded the church porch on Christmas Eve.

And at home, when the Mass was over, an immense fire roaring in our bedroom, and Gilbert in the satin dressing gown that brought out the green of his eyes.

The old longing, the present fear, swept over me. No! Don't start to cry! Gilbert would not want you to cry....

†   †   †

The woman shivering in that icy attic room so many years ago was Adrienne de Lafayette; the husband she ached for, the hero of the American Revolution. Thirteen years had passed since Gilbert de Lafayette returned in triumph from the United States, his role in the winning of our independence inscribed forever in our hearts and our history books.

What is not so well-known on our side of the Atlantic is what happened in the remaining fifty years of his eventful life. And still less, the part played in all of this by his wife.

In fact, until I encountered her name on the grave slab next to his in a tiny, out-of-the-way cemetery in Paris, I had not even known that he *had* a wife. Neither, apparently, did most people. "Was Lafayette married?" was the usual response when I tried to learn more about her.

It was enough to get my fairness-to-women flags flying. By then I'd unearthed some facts about Adrienne de Lafayette in dusty library stacks in Paris and Auvergne. I had met a woman every bit as courageous as her husband, a realist while he saw things as he wished them to be. I'd met a home lover who asked nothing but the companionship of her husband and the chance to raise their three children in peace. She was given instead: fame, adventure, and a role in history.

What I learned made me want to know more. Not just because her life was filled with stirring events, but because I was convinced that Adrienne had learned things about living in a time of catastrophic change that we in the final years of *this* century need to know.

For in spite of the immense differences between her world and ours, there are strange parallels, too. The world in which Adrienne grew up was as sophisticated as our own, and a great deal more graceful—probably the most elegant and cultured society the world has ever known. (It was this for the few, of course, not for the many; but Adrienne was one of those few.)

As today, ferment was everywhere—in science, in politics, in heady new ideas about equality and liberation. Many of the fabulously rich, people like Adrienne and Gilbert, were in the forefront of the movement to see the world's goods more fairly divided. Never before had there been such optimism, such faith in human potential. Science was at last revealing its secrets; poverty, disease, injustice would soon be things of the past.

Only a few of those working so hard to bring all this about had private doubts. Adrienne was one of them. She shared her husband's passionate commitment to democracy. She did not share his certainty that it would mean an end to human misery.

Adrienne suspected the existence in mankind of something darker, deeper than laws could reach, something only God could touch. For she was that rarity in 18th-century France, an educated person who believed the teachings of the church. Nobody who was anybody—not even bishops and archbishops—believed all those old dogmas. The peasants did, of course, but that was because up till now they'd been without hope in this world. When unjust laws were repealed and man's natural goodness allowed to express itself, then all these primitive beliefs about God becoming man—and dying on a cross for something called *sin*—would vanish like mist in the sunshine.

But Adrienne, so modern in most things, was stubbornly old-fashioned in this. With her mother and her sister Louise she persisted in attending daily mass and in daily Bible reading and prayer.

There was another way in which she was hopelessly out of step with her day: her view of marriage. Quite ridiculous, of course. She had been betrothed to Gilbert, as was only natural, before they ever laid eyes on one another: unions of the high nobility were not individual decisions so much as corporate mergers.

Love, of course, existed—was preeminent, in France!—but what did that have to do with the business arrangement called marriage? Adrienne was fourteen, Gilbert sixteen, when their marriage was consummated. Soon Adrienne discovered—somewhat to her alarm, earnest young Christian that she was—that she was also a rapturously passionate person. The awkward thing, in 18th-century France, was that the man she loved so desperately was her own husband.

And he loved her. But Lafayette was a hero—and a Frenchman. And French women were the most enticing in the world, and, except for the few like Adrienne, the least attached to their husbands. Gilbert's love for Adrienne was genuine, but it was not exclusive, while hers for him was, along with her love of God, the fixed passion of her life.

Christian commitment in an age that worshipped science, faithfulness in marriage when it was neither expected nor fashionable—Christians at the end of the twentieth century can recognize Adrienne's predicament. And into the midst of these private tensions burst the public upheaval called the French Revolution.

What a lot, I kept thinking, Adrienne would have to tell us about living through violent times. How I wished that I could sit down with her, as I've had a chance to do with outstanding Christians of our own day, to ask the intimate, painful questions.

And then I realized that I could. Whatever else was going on—in peace and in war, by sunlight and candlelight—the people of the 18th-century wrote letters. Physically separated much of their married life, Gilbert and Adrienne wrote each other constantly. They wrote to their parents, their children, their families, their business partners, their servants. And all of these people wrote back.

An astonishing number of these letters survived shipwreck and revolution—to end in those poorly lit library archives. It was there that I began my "interviews" with Adrienne, at first simply sketching a chronology of her life. She was seventeen and already the mother of fifteen-month-old Henriette, when her husband—only nineteen himself—sailed to fight in the American cause. Her second child, Anastasie, was born six months later, before she even knew that her husband's ship had reached the shores of the New World safely. The following winter, while Gilbert shivered in the snows of Valley Forge, little Henriette died in her mother's arms of a childhood disease.

On Gilbert's return from the United States, two more children were born to the young couple: George Washington Lafayette, named for Gilbert's favorite general, and Virginie, for the state where the British surrender occurred. It was Adrienne's dearest wish—and Gilbert's often-stated one—to bring up their three children on his ancestral estate in the peaceful province of Auvergne, in southern France.

Again and again Adrienne made the 400-mile journey to get the château ready. And each time, some new public crisis kept Gilbert in Paris, and Adrienne and the children would return to be near him. The Lafayettes' townhouse on the Rue Bourbon became home away from home for Americans in France, while at the aristocratic French court Gilbert and Adrienne became the most ardent advocates of the fledgling experiment in democracy across the sea.

And slowly, haltingly, France's own experiment in democracy got underway. Gilbert was elected to the national assembly, the first representative body in France in 150 years. With the other assemblymen he plunged into the staggering task of converting an absolute monarchy into a constitutional one.

As the months of debate and speech-making went on, however, the poor of Paris took to the streets in a kind of hysteria of hope too long deferred. Looting, burning, lynching—it was clear that only military force could put down the riots.

But who could command such a force? He would have to be a nobleman, or the officers would not follow. And a friend of liberty, or the common soldiers would rebel. Lafayette was the one man in France sufficiently esteemed by both sides. Mounted on a milk-white horse at the head of his newly formed National Guard, he restored order to the capital, safeguarded the meetings of the assembly, protected the king and queen from the mob.

Coaxing her children to sleep to the sound of gunfire in the streets, Adrienne's heart sang with pride. The whole world at last saw her husband as she did: the gallant knight on a white horse, the perfect hero.

It was her one lapse into idealism. About everything except the man she loved, Adrienne was a realist. She knew all too well that the perfect hero was performing his deeds in an imperfect world.

Lafayette did not know it. When the Constitution was at last

complete—approved by the Assembly, signed by the king—he
believed that the job was done. At that moment he was the most
powerful man in France. But he had as his ideal his commander-in-
chief in the American struggle. As George Washington, victory
won, had refused the title of king and retired to Mt. Vernon as a
simple private citizen, so Gilbert hastened to give up all military
and civil authority.

Once more, Adrienne packed her household into coaches and
carriages for the long journey to Auvergne, "this time, ma petite
Adrienne, for good."

"For good" lasted two and a half months.

Autocratic governments all across Europe were threatening to
invade the new democracy; Frenchmen were summoned to defend
the homeland. On his white horse Lafayette galloped north to take
command of the army near the presentday Belgian border.

What he did not realize was that in the few weeks since his
"retirement," the political picture had continued to change.
Forgotten were the lofty and equitable laws he and the others had
hammered out with such care; the revolution which he had helped
to set in motion was sweeping on. This was not America, with its
self-sufficient frontiersmen and independent farmers. This was
France, a nation of landless peasants and wretched city-dwellers.
Lafayette's sublime, all-reforming Constitution was just so many
words on paper.

To his army camp came the news that the king and queen had
been arrested and placed in prison. As individuals, Lafayette did
not admire Louis XVI and Marie Antoinette. As an institution, he
disliked the whole idea of monarchy. He personally had wanted a
republic under an elected chief executive, as in America where his
beloved Washington was now president. But the Constitution
named the king as head of the state. And Lafayette believed that
the Constitution mattered.

When he asked his troops to pledge loyalty to the king, he was
charged with treason. A few hours ahead of the agents sent to bring
him to Paris for trial and execution, he escaped across the border.

Into the arms of an Austrian patrol. Hated now in France as a
king-lover, he was loathed in the rest of Europe as a revolutionary.

He was incarcerated in Namur, moved to Nivelle, from there transferred, some said to Wesel, some Magdeburg, then—rumor had it—to Olmutz in far-off Moravia. But nobody knew, nobody could say for sure, whether he was alive or dead.

And meanwhile in France the Terror took shape. Any member of the "former nobility" was automatically suspect of anti-revolutionary sentiments. Adrienne was at first kept under house arrest in the château in Auvergne, later in a local jail where at least a sympathetic turnkey permitted her children occasional visits. Eventually, however, she was transported to Paris and placed in one of the prisons that were mere waiting-rooms for the guillotine. The king was beheaded in January 1793, the queen the following October. Twenty thousand men and women mounted those same wooden steps, among them Adrienne's mother, who had devoted her life to deeds of charity, her deaf and senile old grandmother, and her beloved sister Louise.

Only the appeals of the American ambassador kept Adrienne from the same sentence. "Her name is revered in America," James Monroe reminded government authorities.

And then France itself recoiled from blood and horror. In August 1794 the radicals were overthrown, replaced by a more moderate group of revolutionaries. The remaining nobility were released from prison, while into jail went the radicals themselves, along with black marketeers and other lawbreakers, in the sweeping reforms carried out by the new government. The population of the prisons made an almost total turnabout—except for the woman who bore the name Lafayette. Extremists on both sides hated that name—but so did the new moderate leadership. Compromise, adjustment, bending of principles was their approach, and Lafayette had repeatedly refused to give an inch on principle.

But, after all, since the start of the Terror thousands of French women had dropped their married names. In September a little committee from the new regime visited Adrienne in prison to inform her that she could be released immediately under her maiden name . . . her mother's name . . . any name in the world but Lafayette. "And as your husband is in all probability dead, Citizeness. . . ."

"I believe my husband to be alive, sirs. And if he is not, then I will bear his name all the more devotedly."

Brave words, in sunny September. But now it was midwinter, the coldest in memory, with freezing rain gusting through the broken window. Had she regretted them? I wondered as I gazed at the portrait of a diminutive woman with prematurely grey hair and large, brooding eyes.

I imagined myself putting that question to her, heard her indignant: "No! Never! Not for a single minute!"

"Not even at night? I can see how you could get through the days, writing letters, keeping busy. But those dark, endless nights!"

"I had memories, you see, of joyful nights."

"And yet the memories themselves must have been painful? So much was lost. So much had changed."

"Yes. Yes, thinking of the past could bring on those hateful tears. And thinking of the future was worse! But there was another way, you see . . . the best one. I discovered it that Christmas Eve."

"Yes, you were telling me about that night . . ."

She would close her eyes, remembering. Remembering that little room on the top floor of a house-turned-prison. . . .

†   †   †

The straw was scratchy beneath my legs. It had grown so dark I could see nothing but the white candle-stubs on the chair seat. How many hundreds of candle-ends, longer than these precious two, would our servants toss away every morning in the great house where I grew up!

If I could not think about my husband without starting to cry, I would think about Christmas Eve in that house. I saw the chandeliers in our entrance hall showering light from a thousand crystal prisms, and myself, age seven, dressed for my first midnight Mass at the church of St. Roch across the street.

Louise, age eight, tied a fur-trimmed bonnet over her dark curls, while Mama's wide, wide skirt preceded us out the door. Our major-domo led the way across the broad forecourt, aglow with lanterns, his tall staff tap-tap-tapping on the marble pavement. In the street beyond, it looked as though all the poor of Paris had gathered. There were always beggars outside our house, for Mama's generosity was known, but never so many as this—snatching off their caps, thrusting their hands almost in our faces. We were on foot because Mama would never be carried in her traveling chair to church. "Our Lord walked the dusty streets when He was on earth. Are we to set ourselves above Him?"

"The Countess!" the people cried. "Alms, Madame la Comtesse! Alms for the birth of the sweet Savior!"

The major-domo distributed the coins from Mama's purse, then started up the steps into the church, tapping, tapping with his ivory staff.

I sat up straight. Surely I had really heard that! Tap, tap, tap . . . there it came again—the floor below!

I sprang to my feet and felt for the door. A murmur of conversation rose from five floors below as I groped down the black corridor. Again, three short taps! "Citizen carpenter!" I hissed down the dark stairs. "Up here, that leak in the roof! Up here!"

"Ah, one moment, Citizeness! It is so dark. . . ."

That voice I had known since childhood! Now I heard his footsteps on the steep, narrow stairs. Reaching out, I found his hand. I led him swiftly down the lightless corridor to my room, and soundlessly closed the door behind us.

He raised my fingers to his lips. "Madame la Marquise!"

"Your blessing, Reverend Father!"

The forbidden titles seemed to ring in the night air, although we had spoken in whispers. And then titles were forgotten as we embraced. "Praise God!" the old man kept saying. "Praise God for his goodness!"

For my part, I was too shocked to speak. Beneath his workman's smock my arms encircled not the portly, comfortable figure I remembered, but a skeleton clothed in skin. Could this be the good Pere Carrichon, the round-cheeked priest who was forever popping the buttons down the front of his cassock?

"Your children are well, Madame! I bring messages. . . ." Of family and friends he had much welcome news. Only of my husband, only of Gilbert did he know nothing.

Suddenly I could bear the darkness no longer. I had to light at least one of the candles, after so many months of seeing only the faces of strangers. I groped for the chair, found the larger of the two little stubs, and felt on the floor for the tinderbox. Whether from cold or excitement my hands shook so that I could hardly strike a spark. At last the candle caught. I lifted it toward him . . . and caught my breath.

If it had not been for his voice I would have thought there was some awful mistake. The good-natured ruddy face I remembered was ash gray, the skin of the cheeks hung in folds. His hair which I recalled as gray and close-cropped, was shoulder length and quite white. Pere Carrichon could not be more than sixty; the man in front of me looked eighty.

"Dear friend," I began—and then saw that he also was staring in disbelief. Had I too, then, changed so very much?

The old man's horrified gaze traveled from me to the spartan little room: the single chair, the straw-filled pallet. "Is this—where you live, my lady?"

"I requested this room, Father. In the large ones below they put eight or nine people. Here I can write, I can pray."

"Your pardon, Madame la Marquise. I did not mean to question the all-seeing providence of God. It was just that, for a moment, comparing this room with—"

Both of us froze. Loud voices rang out somewhere below. A shout and then a crash . . . a fight, no doubt. They broke out often during the long supperless evenings. There was still no sound here on this floor, but it was a reminder of how swiftly our moments together might end.

Hastily we turned to the makeshift communion table. Pere Carrichon unwrapped several loops of a long, ragged scarf from around his neck and with an apologetic smile draped it evenly down the front of his carpenter's smock, making of it a priestly stole. With the lighted candle he lit the other and placed them on either side of the wooden "chalice."

Now he rummaged in his leather sack and drew out a hammer and nails. "If someone comes, you must pick up the candles as if you were lighting my work, and fold the shawl over the rest." Then he raised his hand in blessing:

"Dominus vobiscum," he whispered.

"Et cum spiritu tuo," I replied.

Turning back to the chair he launched into the ancient liturgy. "Te Deum laudamus. . . ."

As the rhythmic Latin phrases poured into the little room, I closed my eyes and sank to my knees. I did not see the wooden bowl and the black bread on the woolen shawl. I saw the high altar at St. Roch, its golden vessels glimmering . . .

So rapt in the well-remembered scene was I that I did not realize that Father Carrichon had stopped speaking. I opened my eyes to see him looking at me in puzzlement. "We confess our sins to Almighty God," he repeated.

Yes, of course, he was awaiting my response. What were the Latin words that summed up all guilt, all remorse? It had been so long. . . . There! I had them. I opened my mouth to speak the stately Latin formula, but what came out was a rush of ordinary words.

"Father, I failed him! I failed my husband! I did not know how to keep his love! And now it's too late—he may be dead, he—"

"My child! My child!" the old priest broke into my outburst. "Your Father in heaven knows the griefs of your heart. If you are in any way at fault, make your confession and he will forgive you."

I clasped my hands together, trying to steady my thoughts as well. "Lord," I began in Latin, "I am heartily sorry for having offended you. . . ." Swiftly the ancient words worked their healing calm. And now the holiest moment of the Mass had come. Pere Carrichon raised the bread high above his head, asking the Lord of life to enter this attic room. I swallowed the bitter black loaf, and it was the Bread of Life. I touched my lips to the wooden bowl, and it was the Cup of Salvation.

Afterwards, when the final prayers of praise and thanksgiving were said, when Pere Carrichon had drawn off his stole, we embraced again for the sheer joy of our great celebration. One of the candles wavered, flamed briefly, and went out; perhaps another five minutes of light remained in the other.

Pere Carrichon fixed his care-rimmed eyes on mine. "Dear Madame la Marquise, these alarms and regrets for your husband are not the product of faith. Can you not commit him, past, present and future, to God's never-failing care?"

"I do, Father. Every day, every hour. And God tells me that I must go to him! If ever I'm released from this hateful place, it will be to search the world until I find him! Wherever he is, in prison, in a hospital—in the grave—at his side is the only place on earth I can be happy!"

"My dear lady, I tell you again that these transports of passion are not the fruit of submission to God's will. What of your three children, praying daily on their knees that you will be restored to them?"

"They are never for a moment out of my mind. But they do not need me, Pere Carrichon, as my husband needs me."

"Not need you! Why, Mademoiselle Virginie cannot be more than twelve!"

"Dear Father Carrichon, must I quote your own words back to you? The ones you spoke to *my* mother when she had smallpox, and the doctors despaired, and she wept at the thought of leaving her children?"

He shook his head. "I don't recall them. And I don't see how you can. You were only a child."

"But Mama quoted them often to us, afterward. And I have repeated them to myself every day I've spent in prison."

"What were these wonderful words, then?"

"You said to her, 'Do you think you are so indispensable to God that he cannot provide all your children will ever need, both for their bodies and their souls, whether you are there or whether you are not?'"

"Well . . . and very truly said it was! But, Madame, does the same wisdom not apply to your husband? Why can you trust God for your children's welfare and not for his?"

"Because—" How could I explain to Pere Carrichon what I did not understand myself? My children would find God, each in his own way, of that I felt sure. As for Gilbert . . . "Because he trusts only in reason. He believes human beings can be made perfect. He thinks we can create paradise ourselves, without—"

Blackness sprang between us as the second candle guttered out. "I have stayed too long!" Pere Carrichon exclaimed. "I must go!"

Our time was over, and neither of us had spoken of the tragedy looming blacker than the night around us. I groped for my friend's hand in the dark. "Pere Carrichon, they wrote me you were there when Mama and Grandmother and Louise . . . they said you followed the cart."

His hand tightened on mine; he did not answer.

"You were there?" I persisted.

"I was there."

"And were they—did you . . ."

"I saw it all," he said, "and someday I will tell you all, dear, dear lady. But not tonight. Not on the eve of our dear Lord's birth when your mind is distressed with many things. You must not think of the past tonight!" He dropped my hand to search in the dark for his hammer and tool bag. "When you are well, Madame! When you are free and far from this dismal Paris—then will be time to speak of such things."

"But . . . will such a time ever come?" I felt my courage deserting me as he moved toward the door. "The future seems as terrible as the past . . . in the nighttime."

"Do not think of the future, lady! The future is God's. Do not occupy your mind with it!"

"But, dear friend and father, if I may not think of the past, and must not dwell on the future—what is left?"

"Why . . . everything is left, lady! God is left! Do you not know that God exists only and eternally in the now? God exists today—not yesterday, not tomorrow—and as long as you live in the present, you live in him."

Footsteps in the corridor made us both catch our breath. "I will try," I whispered.

Once again his lips brushed my fingers. Then the door opened, closed, and I was alone. I listened at the door with pounding heart, heard his "Good evening, Citizen," as he passed someone in the dark hall, then his footsteps descending the stairs. Nothing else. No sound, no outcry of challenge.

I crossed to the outside wall and stood at the shattered window, straining for the sound of the street gate opening. How silent the city had become! No clatter of hooves in the rue Notre Dame des Champs; no sound of footsteps. The creak of rusty hinges, the slam of the gate! Then no further sound from the strangely quiet street. Dear God, protect your servant! A carriage lumbered past, oddly muffled.

I felt for the chair, set the empty wooden bowl on the floor and drew the shawl once again around my shoulders. Then I knelt on the pallet for my evening prayers. Don't think of the future! Don't remember the past. God exists today.

But . . . how often and how clearly I had seen God this day! If once more no news had come of my husband, at least there was no bad news either. And that meant—that had to mean—that he was alive. And Pere Carrichon had come, God himself had come, to this small room tonight.

I wrapped the shawl tighter, wrapped myself in the wondrous Christmas gift Pere Carrichon had left behind. Christmas was not a long-ago event. Christmas was now. Once more you have come in the dark and cold of night, Lord Jesus! Once more straw has been your bed. . . . You know how it scratches and gets in the nose. The very earth is hushed tonight because you have come.

A feather-soft presence blew in at the window and caressed my cheek, and I understood the strangely silent night. The dismal rain had turned with nightfall to snow. God's pure white covering lay over the bloodstained streets, his Christmas benediction over our heartsick world.

†   †   †

Adrienne was released from the Maison Delmas in 1795. Although ill, she refused the asylum of her home in Auvergne, staying on in Paris until she could arrange to send fifteen-year-old George Washington to the care of his namesake in America. By then she knew reliably that her husband was imprisoned in the fortress of Olmutz, in Moravia. With her two young daughters she made the difficult trip across Germany and Austria, winning from

Emperor Francis II the only thing on earth she desired: to share her husband's cell.

She found Lafayette wasted and ill from three years' solitary confinement. With Anastasie and Virginia she nursed him back to health, in spite of appalling conditions. Not for another two years were the four of them finally set free.

Lafayette and the two girls speedily recovered from the effects of their harsh captivity. Adrienne—ill when she entered Olmutz—did not. For the remaining eight years of her life she suffered blood poisoning, impaired breathing, swollen and painful arms and legs. None of it altered the joy she felt each day she could spend at her husband's side.

They were still all too few. Lafayette remained persona non grata in France. The family settled in Holland while Adrienne, ill and lame, traveled repeatedly to Paris on behalf of family, friends, former servants, and the family's innumerable creditors. In Paris she located Pere Carrichon, who had survived his dangerous role as a priest-in-hiding, and in 1802 officiated at George Washington Lafayette's marriage.

After months of secret inquiry she also succeeded in locating the mass grave where 1300 headless bodies, including those of her mother, sister, and grandmother, had been unceremoniously dumped. With other relatives of the victims she arranged for a wall to be built around the tragic site and daily prayers to be recited in an adjacent chapel.

Adrienne died, surrounded by her family, on Christmas Eve 1807. She was buried in a plot next to that hallowed wall. Her husband lived to play a part in the peace that followed Napoleon's defeat at Waterloo, to tour the United States half a century after independence, to resume command of the National Guard after the Revolution of 1830. Twenty-seven years after Adrienne's death, honored by two nations, loved by innumerable beauties, Gilbert was laid to rest beside the woman who had loved him best.

FIVE

Johanna Lind Hult

by Ingrid Trobisch

HER ONLY CLAIM TO FAME was a photograph of herself on the front page of the *New York Herald Tribune* on Monday, May 19, 1941. It was also the darkest day of her life. Two of her children, a son-in-law, and three grandchildren were reported to have gone to their graves off the coast of Africa. They had been travelling on an Egyptian ship which was sunk by a German raider. It is of such tragedies that news is made.

I remember the events of the day well, for she was my grandmother and I lived through them with her. One of the passengers reported lost was my own dear father.

A sophomore in high school, I was dismissed from classes so that I could be with her. Calm and controlled, she listened to the radio reports hour after hour on that black Monday. At the age of seventy-seven she was by nature an energetic little woman with hands that didn't know how to be idle. She had acquired the discipline of "just being quiet" with difficulty.

The words of farewell she spoke to my father just a month before came back to me. Her head barely even with his shoulders, she had looked up at him and said: "Ralph, remember when you left for Africa that first time, more than twenty years ago? I told you then it was the happiest day of my life. Today I want to say the same thing again."

Now the radio was telling her that she had lost not only a son but also a daughter, and all of her daughter's family.

That day was the longest I had ever lived through. The late news brought us the thinnest ray of hope, suggesting that some passengers may have survived and been taken aboard a prison ship.

The next morning I awoke to the ringing of the phone. As I picked up the receiver, I heard the operator say: "Long distance calling."

An unfamiliar voice came on: "This is Dr. Swanson from mission headquarters in Minneapolis." Why was he calling me? I wondered. Then he said: "We've just received good news from the United Press. Your father is alive and safe! So are your aunt and uncle, and all the other missionaries and passengers. Will you tell your mother and your grandmother?"

Black Monday had given way to a Tuesday of good tidings! The sun was shining. Birds were singing in the maple trees. The world went round and round. It was like Easter joy.

My grandmother's face was serene as she heard the message. It was a serenity that told of suffering overcome.

My earliest memory was of finding refuge in my grandmother's house. It was to me a place of security, love, and warmth.

My parents had returned from their mission post at Moshi, Tanzania, on the slopes of Mt. Kilimanjaro in East Africa. I was born there just in time to make a long boat trip through the Red Sea, the Mediterranean, and then to Sweden. Here we spent a wonderful three months, which brought healing of body, mind, and soul to my battle-worn parents. Along with my two older brothers, I kept them well-occupied. When we reached the States, we settled in Wahoo, Nebraska, where my father did deputation work for the mission.

I am told that I cried often as a young child. My parents rarely picked me up to comfort me since the rules of child-rearing advised against it. I have often wondered if that "weeping child," which my husband said he sometimes detected in me, would have been healed earlier if my mother had ignored the "experts." By the time her last child arrived, she had forgotten those rules and had learned to listen to her own inner mother-voice. At any rate, it must have been a difficult time, and my grandmother, living next door, realized it. She took me in from time to time, and I had "only child" status in her home.

My playthings were stored in a box tucked underneath the legs of her electric stove. The stove was a table model, under which I found the quietness and shelter I needed. After a period of "hiding out" under her watchful eye, I was ready to return to the company of my brothers and my new baby sister. Perhaps that is what grandmothers do best—taking each child separately and giving them the individual attention that a busy mother cannot always provide.

The bond that began to be forged in these first years of my life was completed when I lived with her for two years as a young teenager. I loved her with a love founded on deep respect. Now, four decades later, I realize that her life has formed the pattern for my own. She has become for me, consciously or unconsciously, the model on which I base my life.

My grandmother, Johanna Lind Hult, affectionately known as Tilda, was born in Sweden as the Civil War was drawing to a close in the United States. Her father, Svante Lind, born in a humble tenant home near Skara, Sweden, had a lively sense of humor, which his daughter was to inherit. Her mother, Anna Kajse Larsdotter was born in the city of Skara in somewhat more comfortable circumstances than her future husband. But her father lost the family property when in good faith he signed a note for a friend which dragged them into poverty.

This misfortune prevented Anna from completing school. However, she had a great talent for music and was invited to sing at elite parties of noble families. Since she was not of the noble class herself, she was requested to sing off stage and stand behind a curtain. Eventually, she took a job as a household maid at Harlunda where Svante worked as a hired man. Before long he had fallen in love with the pretty redhead. Anna's mistress presented her with a wedding dress and prepared her for her upcoming marriage. After their wedding in 1856, Svante had to join the

Swedish army and the young couple moved into a small house. The rent amounted to two days of his soldier's pay per week. He kept his own little garden plot which he worked with his milk cow.

Thirteen years later he fled from the army service, since it was impossible in those days to get permission for a release. He sold the family cow and scraped together enough for his passage to America, promising God that he would eventually send for his family and that he would pay back every cent of the money he had borrowed for the trip.

As he travelled across England by train, his knapsack with his food and all his clothes for the voyage fell off the top of the train. Months later he arrived in Hampton, Illinois, where he worked in the coal mines earning enough to pay his debts and the passage to America for his family. Finally, he wrote to his wife in Sweden, advising her to sell the household goods, and even the precious loom which had helped her earn an income by weaving fine linens and selling them. Unfortunately, Svante was not a good business man. He ordered the tickets from a swindler who never delivered them to Anna and the five children.

The impoverished family had to move out of their little house to a yet smaller one and work by the day. The older children were forced to beg. Rye porridge, dark bread, and turnips were often all they had to eat. It was some time before Svante realized that he had been cheated. When Anna's letter came, explaining that no tickets had arrived, he had to start all over again earning their passage. At last he succeeded. Three years after his arrival, on June 17, 1872, he welcomed his family to their new home, a cabin in Hampton Hills, East Moline. Then, in 1879, the family moved to Phelps County, Nebraska, where Svante built a two-room sod house.

Johanna Mathilda Lind, born March 23, 1864, was eight years old on the trip to America. She grew to be a happy and generous child, who loved to help her mother take care of her baby sister. As a young girl she left the family home in Nebraska for a time to attend school in Illinois. She told her mother that the only thing better than going to school in Illinois was rocking her little sister to sleep. But in less than three years the little schoolhouse she attended went up in smoke. The end of the schoolhouse spelled the end of her formal education. From then on she had to work for her living. In Moline she found jobs helping professors and friends from the church where she took confirmation instruction. Though her formal education was limited, she was a bright girl, and she learned much from her contacts with educated people. But before long she was called back to Nebraska.

Her mother had fallen from a ladder and broken her arm at the wrist. Tilda was needed at home. By now she had become a pretty young woman. Bachelors were plentiful and she had quite a few admirers. Before long, she became engaged to a gifted young student who preached at their church one Christmas. He arranged for her to stay with a pastor's family so that she could learn the duties of a pastor's wife. So it was back to Illinois for a time. Shortly after she returned in 1884 her fiance died of tuberculosis. Her youthful hopes were crushed. It seemed that the way of life that was opening before her had suddenly collapsed, just as her hopes for an education had been demolished with the destruction of the schoolhouse. Once again, she took her misfortune in a "stately" mood, as the Swedes would say. God must have other plans for her life.

The Lutheran Church in Kearney was now built and Tilda attended all the meetings and services. A young man by the name of Henry Hult was also a faithful attender. One day Henry asked Tilda's brother-in-law, who frequented the hardware store where he worked, whether she would be interested in forming an acquaintance with him. When her brother-in-law posed the question to Tilda, she simply replied, "Let him ask me. I will give him the answer myself."

Henry and Tilda's wedding took place at her parent's home on the 28th of August, 1887. A comfortable bower was built for the festivities because the sod house was too crowded. Six witnesses stood up for them. "When all had been fed, a powerful thunder and lightning broke loose," writes one of the relatives. "And the water stood like a lake upon the yard. The guests gathered in several small groups. We had to vacate the leafy bower since the roof didn't keep out the rain. But the guests were happy. At the time it was quite an aristocratic wedding." Tilda's younger sister Ida adds these details: "Father and the boys made a frame out of tree branches, a sort of canopy. Benches and chairs were brought from church, and tables were set in the sod home. Mother cooked a whole lamb in the wash boiler, which we ate with potatoes, vegetables, and lemon pie. Augusta and I sang, 'Farewell dear sister.' We had new pink sateen dresses with a small design in the material. Very pretty, of course. Tilda had sewed them."

The newlyweds made their home in Kearney. It was here that their first son, my father, was born on July 9, 1888. They named him Ralph. The heat was terrible, but since so many people were dying of swamp fever (malaria) Henry had asked Tilda to keep the windows closed. He didn't want his wife and child to be infected. She suffered more from the heat than from anything else, she said.

Both parents had dedicated Ralph to the Lord even before he was born. They prayed that he would be a pastor, and, later, God heard their prayers.

Even as a young wife, Tilda was active with her husband in their church. They both taught Sunday School, taking turns so that one could teach while the other watched the little ones in their growing family.

One of my aunts describes Henry and Tilda: "Both Mother and Father were deeply spiritual. Church attendance was an accepted rule, and only sickness kept a member of the family at home. Family devotions were a regular part of our lives at home. Every day began and ended with moments at the family altar. Both our parents served God with deep devotion. Father served on church boards and just before his death was elected to the Luther College Board.

"Good literature and learning were also part of our home life. Mother practically went through school with us, reading history, geography, and other of our textbooks. Father would often read aloud for Mother's benefit, as she was busy knitting, mending, or sewing.

"Father was a man of discipline. He was a man of order and care. But he was also loving and tender. Whenever one of us had a birthday, we had a special treat in store—the birthday child would climb into Father's comfortable lap during morning devotions.

There was no better place. At Christmas he was a child along with us."

In August, 1907, Henry and Tilda moved to Wahoo so that their children could be educated at Luther College. By now they had five sons and three daughters. However, Henry did not live to see his hopes fulfilled. He had gone back to Kearney again to see that his pledge to give the first wagonload of wheat to missions was carried out. This accomplished, he was riding in the wagon which had been used to haul the wheat to the elevator. The horses became frightened and ran wild. Henry fell to the ground and landed on his back. Peritonitis set in after he reached home in Wahoo. He died at home, October 28, 1907.

Their marriage had lasted for twenty years. At the age of forty-three Tilda was a widow with eight children, from the ages of two to nineteen, to raise alone. Again her dreams went up in smoke. Within weeks after Henry's death, her third son died of peritonitis after a ruptured appendix. Shortly after, her brother John, a bachelor who planned to come and live with her and the children, died the next spring. Three deaths within five months—and yet she refused to give up.

She remained in Wahoo, as Henry would have wanted, so that her seven children could be educated there. My aunt describes these years: "Soon after Father's death, Mother bought a house on the western edge of Wahoo. It had four acres, a barn, and a good house. Just north of this was a ten-acre apple orchard. Mother purchased this too. She was determined that none of us would have to quit school. It was Father's wish that we all be educated in our church school, Luther College.

"Mother worked hard. We always had plenty of good meals, we were well-dressed. She made many of our dresses out of good used clothes that Aunt Lou sent us. Mother would rip them and wash the cloth, careful to preserve any of the lovely trimmings which could be used again. She used apples in every possible way, canning and drying them for winter. She had two cows, whose calves she would sell to the local butcher. She also raised a litter of pigs to sell each year, feeding them completely on apples (not a kernel of corn). She also sold milk and cider that we made on our own cider press.

"We were never hungry or in need, even though the crop yield was minimal some years. We had a wonderful place to live. Throughout her thirty-eight years as a widow, Mother kept a happy and good home for us children."

One of her nephews said of her: "She spoke so advisedly, always with a deep and natural Christian accent." She was a living example of Proverbs 31:25-26:

> Strength and dignity are her clothing, and she laughs at the time to come. She opens her mouth with wisdom, and the teaching of kindness is on her tongue.

During the time that I lived with her, she taught me that all Saturday work—cleaning, baking, preparations for Sunday—must be finished by noon. This was her unswerving rule. Then, as she told me, "I go to my bedroom and close the door. My Lord and I have time to fellowship and I study His word." On Sunday morning she would stand in front of the young people's class at church, and they would listen to this wise woman. She spoke out of her long experience, and her words carried authority. One of her former students wrote this about her: "Mrs. Hult—I don't even know her first name—in the 'old days' women weren't called by their given names. I can just picture her walking so stately and dignified, a beautiful woman with a soft speaking voice. She was one of those pioneer women who gave us so much. What a rich heritage we have and how I thank the Lord for it!"

My grandmother took pride in her appearance. I heard her called the best-dressed lady in church. For a poor widow, she was very elegant, because she had a sense of creativity, especially when it came to decorating her hats and remaking her dresses. She was a lady in the best sense of the word, great in the art of self-acceptance. She had learned the secret of Simone de Beauvoir's words: "It is the task of every woman to forget herself, but how can she do that if she doesn't know who she is? Some women never learn to know who they are; and that's why they have so little to give others." My grandmother knew who she was, and this made her one who could speak wisely and with authority.

After the death of her husband, son, and brother she would sometimes express her sorrow by playing Swedish hymns on the organ. Many of them were based on melancholy folk song melodies. Once when she began to play, her youngest child, not yet four, lay on the rug and sobbed, "Mother, that makes me so sad." She never played them again.

Tilda was a good mother of sons. As a child, I sensed that her four sons, one of them a pastor and the others successful businessmen, were very proud of her.

Her sense of humor endeared her to others and restored perspective in difficult situations. I remember one story she liked to tell about herself. She occasionally suffered from dizzy spells. One day she had an attack of dizziness while shopping. To prevent herself from falling down, she held on tight to the bar outside the store. Only after she recovered and walked on did she realize that she had been standing outside the saloon and holding herself up on the bar meant for drunks.

She was an orderly woman, but not a perfectionist. When I threw the dish towel over the hanger after drying the dishes, she would show me how to fold it carefully, so that the kitchen had a "straightened-up" look. But she knew that "nothing is 100% on this earth," and she could be satisfied when something was less than perfect.

Even in her seventies she was a woman of action. When something had to be done, she did it. I recall travelling with her and my father through the Ozarks. We would see sheds in great disrepair. "Let me out," she told my father. "I'd just like to push that one over."

Instead of deploring a situation, she thought of how it could be bettered. If she saw a fruit tree in our orchard with saplings, she broke them off herself instead of telling someone it should be done.

I remember how she praised my own mother: "Ingrid, no one can prepare a good meal with so little to do it with like your mother." Daughters need to hear these words for they don't always have the perspective of someone outside the home.

My grandmother was seventy-eight when she bade farewell to my father as he set out for Africa, this time never to return. Shortly afterwards my mother became desperately ill. She had tularemia, an infectious disease transmitted by insect bites. In 1942, with few drugs to combat it, the doctors gave her little chance of survival.

My grandmother wrote to us children (I was sixteen, the eldest daughter with seven younger brothers and sisters at home): "When I heard about your mother and how terribly ill she was, I went into my bedroom by myself and pleaded with my Lord for help. I asked Him to spare her if possible. I felt relieved and got the assurance that she would get well."

These words gave me more comfort than if the doctor had pronounced my mother's life out of danger. I had great respect for my grandmother's Lord although I didn't have a personal relationship with him myself at that time.

My younger sister told me of the first letter she received from Grandmother. It came when she was spending a year with one of our cousins in order to take confirmation training and to help in the family of small children. Grandmother wrote: "It's your first time away from home and I know you're lonesome and miss your family, but you're with good people." At the end of the letter was the footnote, "P.S. I'm sending you mittens." It was this tangible sign of her love which comforted her granddaughter the most.

At the time he was leaving the States to go to Africa in the midst of World War II my father wrote to his younger brother: "Have received a wonderful letter from Mother.... That letter means so much to me right now." My father was to die from a heart attack after contracting malaria. He died in Dar es Salaam, Africa. I had to break the news to Grandmother on her seventy-ninth birthday. It was a hard blow for both of us, and I leaned on her strength.

Two years later as I walked home from church with her, she turned to me and said, "Ingrid, this is my last week on earth. Soon I shall be with Henry and with your father, Ralph." There was no sentiment—just a matter-of-fact statement.

We had grown especially close after my experience of faith at the end of my freshman year in college. An avid reader all her life, she shared with me the biographies of the great missionary pioneers. When her eyes were tired, I read to her and knew that deep joy of kinship and mutual understanding that comes from being related on a spiritual as well as physical level.

One of the last days of her life, she called me to her bedside. My two sisters and I had come to sing for her and she had requested the song, "Under His Wings, I Am Safely Abiding." Then she asked me, "Ingrid, you want to go to the Sudan, don't you? You feel that this is your calling, to carry on there where your father did pioneer work—but where he could not stay?" I assured her that this was my wish. "Then may I bless you to this end," she said and laid her hands upon me.

I thought of the promise of Psalm 103:17: "But the steadfast love of the Lord is from everlasting to everlasting upon those who fear him, and his righteousness to children's children, to those who keep his covenant and remember to do his commandments."

I was with her as she died in her home, her children around her bedside. It was the first time that I had seen a loved one departing from this life. There was the gasp for air and then a look of great peace came over her. My nine-year-old sister was with us. Later, she said to me, "Ingrid, I don't know whether to cry or to be happy. I am sad to lose my grandma but I know she's happy now."

Because I saw my grandmother die, I realized that death, for a believer, is not to be feared. Therefore, I did not panic when I saw my own husband, so alive one minute, leave this world for good the next. I could imagine the reunion they must have had—my father, my grandmother, and Walter. Knowing that they are together before God's throne, I sometimes feel as though I have a peephole into heaven, something which keeps me going when things seem difficult here.

Grandmother's words comforted me in my own time of trial at Walter's death. One of my aunts wrote to me then and quoted her, saying, "God never places a burden or sorrow on shoulders unfit to carry them." Certainly her shoulders had been strong enough for sorrows and now mine must be too.

In her last years, Grandmother made me a quilt out of the dresses she had sewn for me throughout the years. It was a labor of love and demonstrated her skill with the needle. She gave it to me knowing that she wouldn't be able to quilt it. Her three daughters sat together the days after her death and finished it for me. It has been on my bed in Africa, Germany, Austria, and now in my home in Springfield, Missouri. Maybe this too is a task of grandmothers—to make things of lasting beauty for their children and grand-children. Still today her tangible love keeps me warm.

After my grandmother's death, one of my aunts said, "How we will miss her prayers for us all, for she's no longer here on earth!" I am convinced that although we are separated in body, we are not separated in spirit and that her blessing is with us even more than before. How often I have felt her invisible hand of blessing as I have undertaken a project which seemed humanly impossible. An Episcopalian friend wrote to me recently that the prayers of the Saints are even more powerful than when they were on earth: "Your dear and much loved husband, Walter, prays for you daily and his prayers and the prayers of the Saints allotted each day to pray for your work sustain you and enable you to do what you must here on earth. Because so few people understand the role that the Saints and loved ones who have gone before us are able to play in the lives of those still on earth, much joy is missed and much appreciation, too, of their regard and interest and help."

Gertrude le Fort has said that men are like monuments. Rarely does a famous man have a famous son, because he is likely to burn himself out in his work. But mothers are like rivers, flowing from one generation to the next. "Like a Gulf Stream," they said about Sarah Edwards, the wife of Jonathan Edwards, and her influence on future generations. The same could be said about my grandmother, with all her pioneer qualities, her steadfastness, serenity, stamina, and strength.

I find myself in the middle of this stream. I can reach out one arm and touch my grandmother, carrying with me her example of courage in the face of sorrow and with the other arm touch my grandchildren and pass on to them the heritage of their great-great grandmother.

SIX

Elizabeth Rooney

by Luci Shaw

THE BELL RANG and the poetry workshop closed with a flurry of final questions. As I gathered my lecture notes together and walked out of the classroom with a group of students, a woman who had been waiting quietly by the door came up to me somewhat apologetically to ask if I would look at one of her poems. I was not surprised. People are always doing this. The poem she handed me was simple and short—nine lines. I read it through twice and felt at once the tingling certainty that this was writing beyond the commonplace. I noted the name typed at the bottom— Elizabeth B. Rooney. For me it was a moment of recognition, not of the name—I had never heard it before—but of a kindred spirit, one whose work had a poetic quality that lifted me out of that noisy, academic hallway at the heart of a writers' conference into the limitless blue of an evening sky patterned with darting chimney swifts:

The chimney swifts cut patterns in the sky.
They snip, snip, snip
Great soaring circles of the hanging blue
And carry them away to line their nests
So fledgling chimney swifts,
Born in the dark, soot-blinded,
Will be reminded of the sky

And know which way to go
When they begin to fly.

I heard myself voicing a remark rare for me: "Mrs. Rooney, this is extraordinarily good stuff! Can I see more of your poems?" Appearing genuinely surprised, though pleased, she handed me two other typed sheets. I read them both through with rising excitement. The first was called "Cream."

From the white depths
The poem's richness rises,
Clotting in thickened skins
Across my soul.

I rise and skim
The spirit-filled surprises
And fill with cream
The paper's empty bowl.

Next was "Eschaton":

I saw the world end yesterday!
A flight of angels tore
Its cover off and heaven lay
Where earth had been before.

I walked about the countryside
And saw a cricket pass.
Then, bending closer, I espied
An ecstasy of grass.

I looked at the writer more closely. Elizabeth Rooney was an unpretentious woman with short, nearly white hair and a face of singular sweetness, tranquility, and strength. In the brief conversation that followed she told me some things about herself which intrigued and moved me.

The most striking fact to emerge was that in August 1978 during her induction into a lay order of Episcopal women known as the

Society of the Companions of the Holy Cross, and during the retreat that had followed, she had experienced a sudden, astonishing joy, an awareness of God's presence and his sweetness that affected her profoundly. "I fell in love with God," she told me simply. "It was as if my veins were bubbling with champagne."

As this spiritual and emotional exaltation grew in the following weeks, she came to realize that she had been supernaturally overwhelmed by the Holy Spirit in a way she had neither expected nor asked for. One of the results was that she began to write poetry, something she had not done since college days.

I asked her about this new gift. "How often do you write these verses? And how many?" "Oh, all the time," she replied with a laugh, "sometimes as many as four or five a day." The amazing thing to me was not only the number of poems she was writing, but their literary quality, their sharply focused intensity, if these samples were representative. They reminded me of Emily Dickinson.

Of course, I thought, this is the sort of thing that *should* happen—first the Holy Spirit's visitation, then the spiritual release spilling into the intellect—the holy overflow resulting in a surge of creative thoughts and images and words. Why was this coalescing of spirit, intelligence, and imagination so rare? I had often been urgently assured by writers who were Christians that "the Holy Spirit gave me this poem," only to be shown writing of such banality or sentimentality, work so stale or derivative, that I blushed for the Holy Spirit. But here was writing that resonated. It was fresh, vivid, richly packed with meaning, imaginative—real poetry. The seed ideas had been *shaped* into works of art. A poet is, by definition, a "maker," one who works the "given" images and concepts into arrangements of words, not just a human CRT on line with the Main Computer.

How had this gentle, unassuming woman been able so spontaneously to combine real faith with creativity? I sensed a mystery at work; the word "mystic" even came to mind. Yet though there was an otherworldly dimension to Elizabeth Rooney, it was fused with a practical earthiness that was appealing—comfortable and comforting.

But other workshops were beginning that afternoon. Our time

was gone. We exchanged addresses and after I asked her to send me more of her writing we said goodbye and blessed each other in Christ's name.

In the following months our contacts were infrequent, occurring in the cracks of our two very crowded lives—a letter or two, a phone call. I realized I knew little about the details of either her present life or her background, but her chimney swifts kept darting through my thinking.

The following winter Elizabeth phoned me one snowy night to say that she was in Wheaton for a trade show (A trade show? This contemplative dreamer?) but that this one evening was free. Could she come over and visit us? "Yes, if you'll bring me some more poems!" A delighted chuckle—she just happened to have some with her! When she arrived, the trade show mystery was solved; she explained that her family farm in Blue Mounds, Wisconsin, overlies a natural underground cave, the Cave of the Mounds, containing scores of limestone formations—a tourist attraction, with a gift shop and restaurant. Elizabeth was at the Dupage County Fairgrounds near us for a Winter Sports Show, to publicize the Brigham Farm cross-country ski trails, newly developed for winter tourists.

That evening, with an oak wood fire blazing in our family room fireplace, we spread out her poems on the couch and began to explore together the shared country of the spirit and the imagination. We discovered how much we have in common, our acquaintance with and deep admiration for people like Madeleine L'Engle and Winifred Couchman, our wholehearted response to the created world that greenly surrounds us both, our passionate love for good literature, our perfectionism—the compulsion to get things *right*, our vulnerability to the demands of other people's needs, our hunger for personal approval and acceptance, our fascination with the metaphysical poets, our equivocal responses to the constant pulls from several directions—God, family, vocation, occupation (to put it another way—from prayer, people, writing, and daily work).

It was an evening rich with shared realities. I confessed to her my delight at finding, at our first meeting, a Christian whose writing seemed to flower so naturally out of closeness to God and nature—human and otherwise—that there seemed to be no dichotomy between faith and art. We discussed how poetry rises most authentically from the events and impressions of ordinary life, the specifics—what C.S. Lewis called "the tether and pang of the particular"—and in a letter following our time together, Elizabeth quoted to me a current entry from her journal: "The more I strive for pure holiness, the more I am plunked back into the ordinary—the miracle of rain and of green, the essential toadness of a toad. Yes, the end *is* the beginning but with this difference—at the end you comprehend the sacramental quality of the beginning and rediscover that though ordinariness is all there is, ordinariness is no longer ordinary, it is, rather, sacred and infinitely significant. The carrot I peel is no longer merely a carrot."

In a later letter she commented on the arrival of poems: "Mine seem to come like butterflies, and I try to net them and get them on paper without knocking too many bright bits of color off their wings. My problem is to know how to improve them without destroying them. I do hope they can open to me more friendships like yours and chances to tell people about the Lord to whose love we all respond."

As Elizabeth Rooney continued to send me new poems and as we discussed ways to strengthen them further, I encouraged her to share them with a wider circle. She had already been urged to do this by friends and critics such as Margaret Sheets and Virginia Huntington. But her hesitation is typical of new poets. "I must confess I feel timid about sharing my poems with anyone; it's a step toward intimacy, somehow." Coupled with her natural diffidence was the problem of finding quiet time to write and rewrite, let alone time to type and retype, then submit the work to editors. There was also the sense that a precious, private vision would, in the process of publication, become commercialized. But gradually she gained confidence that God's gifts of insight are not meant to be guarded and hidden, but broadcast like seeds so that they might root in other fertile minds.

When the opportunity came for me to write this chapter, I knew I wanted to write about a woman who was both Christian and poet.

Rather than telling of the impact on my life of an internationally known personality, I felt a growing conviction that I would rather talk about someone like Elizabeth Rooney, an "ordinary" woman, hardly known beyond her own circle of friends and colleagues, though uniquely gifted by God. Her experience would, I was sure, suggest to other women with earthbound, unremarkable lives that he could lift the most mundane existence into his own beauty and glory. What he requires are eyes open to his brightness and ears alert for his voice.

My discovery of Elizabeth was furthered through the reading of some of her journals, generously lent at my request. Never intended for publication, but written purely as a series of personal reflections, they are diaries of soul-growth rather than historical records, pinning down on paper her day-to-day responses and insights and the seemingly trivial events that might otherwise evaporate and be forgotten. A large proportion of her entries are poems in different stages of composition, often distilling into verse the content of the prose entry for that day. In her small, neat writing she gave me a series of provocative hints and clues to her circumstances, the people she loved, the web of her activities spread between the Cave, her church, her prayer group, her home and family. Even more intriguing was the record of her developing inner life with God.

To fill in some of the gaps in my understanding, I drove the three hours northwest from West Chicago to Blue Mounds through a green and golden day in early May 1982. I recognized the Mounds from several miles away, curving up like two gentle breasts from the rolling Wisconsin terrain that surrounds them. Elizabeth had told me to follow the signs to Cave of the Mounds and to come directly to the Cave to find her. I left my car in the tree-circled parking lot and walked down the sloping track. I liked the cultivated wildness of the landscape, bright with local wild-flowers and alive with the sounds of birds and wind-chimes. The gift shop, ivy-covered, against a low cliff face, was charming, inside and out. (Elizabeth had told me that, as the buyer, she chooses half the kind of gifts she likes herself and half the kind most tourists seem to demand, such as T-shirts emblazoned with the legend "Cave of the Mounds."]

And there I found her, at the back of the shop near the entrance to the subterranean Cave. A warm hug, a "Welcome!" and I felt at home. It was lunchtime, and after joining Mike, her charming, witty, down-to-earth husband, we crossed a sparkling stream to the Brigham Farm Kitchen where we had bowls of the best chili I'd ever eaten, with homemade brown bread. Later I was to go on a tour of the Cave with Mike, but first Elizabeth and I drove up the hill to their home where I was installed in the guest room.

Brigham Farm, high on the side of one of the Blue Mounds, looks south across a green lawn and through a fringe of trees to the barns and outbuildings of the Cave and its surrounding parkland, and over distant levels of fields and forests. It is an old, comfortable, two-story frame house, complete with dogs (Jiggs, Gretel, and Flopsy) and a well-used front verandah with steps good for sitting on in the early morning and drinking coffee. Throughout the house the windows are large and uncurtained ("It's O.K. The people all look out; only deer and trees look in.") A portrait of Ebenezer Brigham, one of the family patriarchs, monitors the large living room with its rich, worn, oriental rugs, shelves overflowing with books, and a wood stove that radiates a warmth as real as Elizabeth's and Mike's.

We sat on the porch steps in the afternoon sun and got down to the important business of discussing life. Our conversation ranged far and dug as deep as time would allow. We found more things in common: we both are the children of older parents and both have had life-changing encounters with the Holy Spirit. Other facts were highlighted in our conversation. Elizabeth grew up in that very house, with parents who were upright, gentle, widely read, and churchgoing. Their daughter's journal notes: "I was too young to realize how exceptional my childhood was. I remember in high school wishing I had ordinary parents who lived in a little brown house in town and went bowling and to the movies instead of parents who lived in a big white house in the country and read poetry and Dickens and the *Atlantic Monthly* aloud to each other and listened to the sermons on the Sunday Evening Club."

They were always quite poor, until the discovery of the Cave on the property began to bring in money from tourists. Elizabeth, who had learned to read at home, started her formal education in the second grade in the two-room country school in Blue Mounds. She was too bright to be happy among her peers, who viewed her as conceited. As she put it, "I was pretty miserable except that I loved to learn."

After she graduated, her class's salutatorian, from high school in Madison, she went East to Smith College. One of her professors there was Mary Ellen Chase, a writer and English teacher who dedicated her book *The Bible and the Common Reader* to Elizabeth and the three other Smith girls who were in her honors seminar when she was writing the book. Miss Chase tried to persuade Elizabeth to make writing her career, but Elizabeth felt she had nothing worthwhile to say, a feeling that changed only as she came to know God many years later.

Her time at Smith was a time of religious growth, however. She discovered the Episcopal Church, was confirmed, and headed the New England Student Christian Movement before graduating Phi Beta Kappa. Later she earned her M.A. in Christian Education from Columbia and Union Theological Seminary. Though she studied under Niebuhr, Tillich, and Van Dusen, she recalls, "I always felt that we were learning about God as if we were learning about algebra. We had brilliant propositional teaching about God, but there was no sense of God as a personal intimate."

Edwin J. Rooney—Mike—entered her life as a student at General Theological Seminary while she was at Union. As soon as they both graduated, they were married and lived, for the next thirty years, in the East, where their four children, Mark, Jonny, Betsy, and Patty were born and where Mike served as an Episcopal priest in several parishes, on the staff of the Diocese of New York, and on the Executive Council of the Episcopal Church.

In 1972 the family moved back to Wisconsin to manage Brigham Farm and the Cave of the Mounds. Elizabeth Rooney, always an active church worker, began her years as an employment counselor, helping disadvantaged youth and welfare clients. She was also a devoted and creative mother. A yellowed, pencilled school report from Patty, then seven years old, reads: "If I did not have my mother I would not be living. My mother has black hair. She mostly wears skirts. She has brown eyes. If I did not have my mother to cook my meals I would starve. My mother helps our house to be happy. She teaches me the things I want to know and should know. She likes to help the hurt people. My mother is a kind person. She loves me and I love her." It was Patty who remarked to her mother as a small child, "Everything you say goes into me and I think about it."

The second day of my visit, Patty's elder sister Betsy—small, sunny, quick, and warmly affectionate—filled me in some more. "Mom always showed us how to climb for things rather than just bringing them within our reach." The children were appreciated by their parents as homegrown friends and eager discussion partners. When I asked Betsy if her mother had any faults she hesitated. Finally, "Mother needs to learn to be angry!" she laughed.

Of course, these biographical facts only skim the surface. Elizabeth had matured beautifully in many areas in her life. Spiritually, however, she felt that she had been "marching in place." Oh, there had been gleams of spiritual insight, moments when God seemed real and close, longings for the freedom of spiritual wings. Her poem, "Wild Geese," echoes this heart cry:

Barking and calling courage to each other,
The singing skein sweeps south across the sky.
We hear their legendary cry
Saying goodbye to summer swamps and sweetness.
They know some ancient mystery of weather,
Of daring and of caring for each other,
Which we have lost.
Shrouded in sheets and city streets,
Our stifled hearts half waken at their sound.
Something within us trembles, flaps its wings,
Falls back against the ground.
We dress for breakfast, start the daily round
And wonder, why
Must we know only fenced yards,
And shelled corn, until we die?

But in God's time came God's initiative—at Adelynrood, in Byfield, Massachusetts. Elizabeth arrived there after a year's probation and study, to become a member of a very special group of lay women—the Society of the Companions of the Holy Cross, whose lives are committed to intercession, thanksgiving, and simplicity of life.

And now, because she has said it all so much more truly and cleanly, firsthand, than I could describe it for her, here are some "bits of bright color" from the butterfly wings of Elizabeth Rooney's journals—excerpts I have chosen thematically rather than in any strict, chronological order.

†   †   †

"How does someone feel when the God of Love moves into her life?" I had wondered. These were some of Elizabeth's first responses:

From her journal entry for August 11, 1978:

"Invite a tornado in and what do you get? You get swept away, that's what—'A mighty, rushing wind.' I hadn't really thought of inviting you in, Lord. I sort of thought I'd just keep handing you bits and pieces of my life, like feeding a tramp at the back door without letting him in to mess up the kitchen. You know and I know that I need to let you in. So here goes everything. . . ."

Her first poem, "Adelynrood":

The winter of my heart
Melts here.
Rivulets run
Beneath the ice of fear.

Pierced by your warmth
Life moves.
Spring has begun.
I feel the sun, the sun!

"I am overjoyed—literally bursting with joy. I could caper like a young lamb, except that, not being a young lamb, I would look ridiculous."

RECRUITED

I didn't mean to get into this army of yours, Lord.
I didn't bargain on joy, and on all of this love.
How do I follow these barely perceptible signals
That frequently seem to be coming to me from above?

I've been a good Christian soldier for plenty of years, Lord,
Careful and steady and dull, always marching in place.
I've made very sure that I never would get any closer,
Never so close as to hear you or look in your face.

I thought we were only supposed to be playing a game, Lord,
There on the shore, asking "What would you have me to do?"
Now nothing about me will ever again be the same, Lord,
And it will be ages and ages before you are through!

"My whole purpose and training has been toward excelling, and certainly part of the joy of all this has been a newfound courage that frees me to excel more than I ever did before. But if I start taking credit for this I betray the situation. I feel presumptuous saying that this is the work of the Holy Spirit, but dishonest if I pretend that good old EBR suddenly, all on her own, got her act together and began writing letters and poetry and saying her prayers and getting dishes done promptly and losing weight and being more hospitable and less critical and needing less sleep. And all of this has, in fact been happening with no effort of will on my part. I've just felt so energized by love and joy that I can't obey quickly enough."

"One thing that makes me feel a little daffy and which I hesitate to admit is that I'm inclined to take God entirely literally. When we make everything symbolic we create distance between ourselves and him and I do think God wants closeness. Somehow, this is an appalling idea! When I think of the awesome majesty of God and then that he wants to know me personally, to share my life, to enter my being, to be part of my simple, domestic, earthbound existence, not just symbolically but literally, I feel so inappropriate for such a friendship."

"He doesn't love me *because of me*—my great loveableness; he loves me *because of him*—his great capacity for love."

"The world today is full of charismatic Christians who have the courage to witness to the Lord. I am tempted to be private and special, holier than them, to accuse them of phoniness, bad taste, lack of discretion—any excuse to avoid identifying myself as one who has been with Jesus. The cock that crew for Peter crows for me."

†

Always a keen observer and lover of nature, Elizabeth felt her response to creation and the commonplace augmented by her new closeness to the Creator:

"I'm so glad God loves color. What a generous distributor of it he is—but also, always the ultimate artist, never picture-postcard color. Vulgarity and Puritanism are alike in denying God—the one, his artistry and restraint, and the other, his joy and exuberance."

"The sun has come over the horizon and the eastern side of every leaf and branch and tree trunk is glistening with gold. I feel like that. I'm always the same twig, but to the extent that I allow myself to be suffused with God as the trees are with sunlight I am transformed, golden and glistening. I don't have to do anything except stay in the same place and be still and let him come."

> All of the bushes are burning now!
> All of the trees are aflame!
> The woods are alive with the glory of God
> And the leaves are telling his name!

"I am trying for simplicity of life and every day gets richer and more peopled, more alive with beauty and tenderness. Mike is so dear and loving, Jonny and Mark and Patty and Betsy so fond and promising; the Companions pour affection into my life; and Grace Church is blossoming with love and prayer. And this benign weather—this gentle, golden Fall! A sunset tonight like a great, rose-colored wing curved over the edge of the world."

JOSEPH

Joseph was a good man.
It's hard to be

A good man here below.
Joseph was true,
True as a tree is true.
He did what the angel
Told him to do.
When Mary needed his shelter,
He was there,
Strong as a tree,
Four square.
Joseph knew how to obey.
We'd call him Joe
If he were living today—
"Hey Joe, can you mend
My hay rack?"
"Why Joe, you've done
a beautiful job on my chair!"
Yes, Joseph was a good man.
When God needed him,
He was there.

"The Baltimore orioles are back—three at least, whistling their triple whistles and flashing in and out among the new leaves, leaves so new that they run through all possible variations of lemon and lime. And the leaves of one oak tree are distinctly and delicately pink. Imagine making something as useful as a tree, as efficient at converting sunlight into food and fuel, as huge and tough as a white oak that can live 300 years, and then decorating it with tiny, pink leaves and pale green tassels of blossoms. Until men can make solar convertors as beautiful and functional as oak trees, we had better remember to feel humble."

†

Did her growth toward holiness and her new clearness of vision negate Elizabeth's individuality and personhood? Emphatically no! Listen to the humanity that vibrates from these entries:

"Today I am—'fifty-four and ready for more!' Mike says I remind him of the *New Yorker* cartoon of the very rich, very fat man kneeling by his bed in his silk dressing gown and saying, 'I want more!'"

"Today I couldn't do anything right and all my pretensions have been pretty well knocked from under me. God knows the pretensions are ridiculous and so he mercifully relieved me of them. But I feel pretty blah, like a pricked balloon. I guess deflated is the opposite of elated."

"Mother used to say regularly, 'What have you done today to justify your existence?' When I told the prayer group this last week, they shuddered visibly. The question epitomizes the pre-redemption dilemma—how do I earn my own salvation? All through school I worked so hard to achieve, to prove my worth, to please my mother. But the goal was self-centered—*my* success, *my* worth.'"

"I know now that I can never justify my existence, or deserve God's friendship. Instead I think about him and am overwhelmed. I want to be as good, as pure, as humble, as useful, as obedient as he can make me—not to justify my existence but to say Thank You."

"The important thing is not whether my will is crossed (lovely verb!) but whether I yield to anger, self-pity, revenge when I am crossed, or whether I can attain gentleness and humility and unselfishness."

"Our old, faithful dog just died within the last twenty minutes. We each work out our grief in our own way. I'm trying to get as much of mine as I can out through words. Jonny has taken a chain saw and retreated into the woods north of the house where he is working his out on the logs."

FARM DOG

The chain saw bites through the skin and flesh of the log.
The sawdust spills bright on the fallen snow,
Bright as the blood of the farmer's favorite dog
When she came staggering back from the road below.

She was already dying, there at the door,
Still wagging her tail, still trusting his love to save her.
He had not known what kind of a morning chore
Awaited him. Still, he was there, and gave her

All of the love that he could—called the vet,
Carried her out to the truck.

They sutured the gaping wound but her heart gave out.
And now he is out in the woods
In his old green coat, tackling the logs for relief—Sawing
and sawing and sawing away at his grief.

"It's so important to live fully. Since grief is my assignment for today, Lord, help me to grieve wholeheartedly, allowing the reality of the grief to possess me until it becomes appropriate to move beyond it."

†

For Christian women with family responsibilities as well as the call to be accountable for a creative gift and its development, there will always be an ongoing conflict. Which stands highest on the priority scale—the urgent or the important? What do you give your time to—God, family, gift, or a needy world? Here are Elizabeth's thoughts, as one finite individual responding to multiple demands:

"We are part of the web of the world and God wants to redeem the whole web. (The cat just threw up and a squirrel has arrived on the bird feeder. Some web! I have also fed Jiggs and the cats, plugged in the truck, and started the dishwasher.) That's in parentheses but it's relevant. These are the realities of the web I'm meshed in and it's not for me to say or feel that it's more important for me to write poetry than to mop up after the cat. There's no doubt about what I'd *rather* do but the important thing is what God would rather I did. Some choices are obvious, but right now, should I get Mike's breakfast or keep on writing? It's 7:50 and I've been writing for three hours. I'll write until 8:00 and then cope with domesticity."

"The trouble with falling in love with you, Lord, is that I miss you so terribly unless I am with you all the time. Looking back I can see I am like Peter in his attempt to walk on water. The minute I begin to hoard anything—my strength, my time, my energy, the pleasures of feeling filled with the Spirit—I lose my peace, begin again to worry and complain. Right down into the water of failure I go."

"Moments of aloneness are so precious. What shall I do first—pray or write? To write without praying seems so precipitate and unblessed and yet, if I always begin with praying when I have so little time for writing, I will never get the writing done at all."

OH, BOTHER!

Why don't you give up, God?
You know me by now—
The churning restlessness,
The worrying, and how
Tense and distracted I am.

You keep asking me
To stop fussing and play,
To relax and rejoice
And admire your new day.
I'm *busy*, Lord.
I have things to do.
Like Martha, I'm never through.

Yes, I know Mary chose
The better part,
Simply stopped still
And opened up her heart.
It's something I'd really
Like to do
But not right now. Right now
I'm much too busy
For you.

"Today I ache all the way from toe to head. Menopause? Accumulated fatigue? Guilt? Evil spirits? I think I'll assume normal accumulated fatigue and just offer the remnants of my energy to the Lord and proceed in low gear for the day. There are a lot of useful things I can get done while in low gear."

"Today I cleaned the orange juice machine. The ironing is undone. We have an ozone alert. Skylab is falling. My feet hurt. Mike keeps asking me to complete the corporation minute book. Betsy looks so tired it hurts. But do these things really matter when I know that the children are moral and good, and believing

Christians, when I know that my Redeemer liveth? I need to learn over and over that the things that are happening to me in this life are the raw materials of which our Lord wants me to build a grace-filled life."

"When I left Adelynrood I was thinking that the poetry was a kind of reward for promising to follow Christ and that I must be very obedient and stick close to him so that the poetry would come. That was getting my priorities exactly backwards. If writing is a means of growing closer to God, lovely, but the goal is not writing but learning to conform my will to his. Maybe he intends me to be a frustrated poet but an obedient wife, housekeeper, ticket seller, and servant for him."

†

But it was becoming clearer to Elizabeth and to those who read her writing that she was not meant to be "a frustrated poet." The poems and insights continued to come, and with them an increased understanding of the role and the craft of the writer:

"I know what I want to say. I want to write about God, about the intense tenderness manifest in the world wherever goodness, truth, and beauty allow it to shine through, about the essence of things— Plato's ideals showing forth not just in the relative dullness of tables but in bicycles and keys and gardens and loving people. (My apologies to tables. They aren't dull either.) I want to keep saying it while it's fresh. The question is, how am I to find the time? I find myself a constant refugee from my family. I love them, need them, want them, but saying my prayers and writing poetry, the two activities of greatest importance to me at the moment, are not communal activities."

"Emily Dickinson wasn't a recluse; she was trying to concentrate."

"Writing is like praying. It doesn't come to much unless you do it every day."

"We saw an old-fashioned copper still in Horse Cave, Kentucky. The mash goes in a tightly covered kettle, a fire burns underneath, steam rises and runs downhill through a covered eavestrough and recondenses as it circulates inside a copper pipe coiled round within a barrel of cold water. The condensed steam comes out a spigot at 180 proof.

"In order to say anything significant, a writer has to operate on much the same principle. All of life's emotions, excitement, stimuli must be contained, brought to a boil, prevented from leaking out in casual conversation but instead distilled and cooled through the writing. If the experiences are rich and the writer both passionate and disciplined and, especially, also skilled with words, he can distill life as he knows it and make of it a heady potion for his readers, a rich liqueur. Writing takes solitude—and not just aloneness filled with housework and busy work and radio. Solitude has to be aloneness in which you allow all the stirred up dust of your thoughts to settle into patterns. Then, you try to describe the patterns."

†

A poet's merit is largely dependent on sensitivity. But sensitivity is openness not only to images and ideas, not only to the music of the spheres and the melody of a single phrase, but to expressions of need in other people's lives:

"'Bear ye one another's burdens and so fulfill the law of Christ.' *We are* one another's burdens and when we relate to someone, we bear *him*, not just his burdens. This concept gives significance to the most casual contact, between the customer in front of the counter and the clerk behind it, the driver waiting for a traffic light and the man in the car behind him. We have a responsibility toward all who touch our lives, even casually."

"I am beginning to learn more about the Cross. I always thought that to walk the way of the Cross meant to seek suffering, and this seemed perverse. I am beginning to realize that it means to learn to love and the more people I love and the more intensely and tenderly I love them, the more opportunities for suffering are presented, as life happens to them and as I learn to share their burdens and care about their cares. Intercession goes well with this because praying for people does make you love them more and more."

"These days it's as if everyone I meet has the potential for becoming a close and dear friend. Is it perhaps by magic that Christians come truly to love their enemies, so instead of your enemies being people whom you hate, they are reduced to being only people who hate you—far less lethal to the soul, regardless of the effect on the body."

"If God can cure someone's cancer, why doesn't he just do it? Why include some human intercessor? I think because the cure, if cure comes, is more beautiful and intricate this way. He prefers to work through us not by force but by asking and waiting and inspiring and hoping. It's the concept of The Great Dance."

†

Ever since Elizabeth's life had been lovingly invaded by God, closeness to him had become not only the central joy but the necessity of her days. And it was in prayer that this closeness was best nourished:

MUTE

Must we use words for everything?
Can there not be
A silent, flaming leap of heart
Toward thee?

"Praying is like swimming. I have trouble getting into depth in either because I am unable or unwilling to let go and trust the element I'm moving in—whether it's water or God. I need to learn abandonment."

"I used to worry when I woke up off schedule, but now I assume that our Lord has something in mind for me, and so I rise and wait."

"Yesterday I patched Jonny's blue jeans instead of saying my prayers because it seemed closer to what God would want."

†

C.S. Lewis talked of moving further up and further in; a phrase that has often come to my mind to describe the divine-human integration is "the in-Godding of man"; however it is described, it involves the increasing intimacy of a love relationship. In her journal and poems Elizabeth Rooney talks of the process of her own growing toward God:

"Virginia Huntington uses the words 'Brim me!' in one of her poems. I think we can be filled with the Holy Spirit quite as literally as a glass is filled with water or a cup with coffee. But you can't pour anything into a cup unless it is held still. We miss the streams of grace, or they miss us, because we can't hold still enough for long enough so God has a chance to fill us with himself."

"God intends us for himself and with our eager cooperation or with our rebellious reluctance he works to achieve this. He respects the reluctance; he will hint and then wait, ask and then wait, urge and then wait. And wait and wait!"

"As I develop an ever-growing, ever-closer relationship with God, immediate mercies are swallowed up in The Mercy, immediate goods are overwhelmed by The Goodness."

"This evening my heart and veins and arteries and my whole system have been filled with a joyousness I can hardly contain. I want to pray or read but feel as though I shall explode. I need to tell someone how wonderful God is!"

I haven't cleaned the cellar,
I forgot to sweep the stair,
There's a button off my jacket,
Jonny's blue jeans have a tear,
There's an old, arthritic lady
Whom I should uphold in prayer,
And I'm sitting in the moonlight,
The moonlight, the moonlight,
Adoring you by moonlight,
As if I had no care!

"Four A.M. I got up and found it had stopped snowing, leaving about a foot of new-fallen snow in great white billows under a full moon. Mike woke up and asked what I was going to do and I said, 'Go to the bathroom,' which was a deception, since after I went to the bathroom I was going to pray and write and wander about as usual. I have to stop lying to people about how much God means to me, just because I'm embarrassed by it or think they won't understand. What if Sts. Peter and Paul had acted like that? Stroke victims have to practice and practice speaking in order to learn to speak again. I need to practice speaking about God, his love, his immanence, his active presence, his willingness to participate in our lives if we'll only let him."

"The story of the talents used to make me feel sick to my stomach because I always identified with the fellow who buried his talent. Now, after this blessed time of total commitment to Christ, I have reread the parable and find I identify with the man who had the ten talents and on whom God kept pouring out more and more good things."

"Reading Catherine Marshall's *Beyond Ourselves* is a great help. It confirms that I have come to admit with considerable timidity, that I did receive the gift of the Holy Spirit during the service when I was admitted as a Companion and that all these perceptions and emotions and sensations and guidings which have marked my life since are not just fantasies and symptoms of mental illness on my part (I have never felt more whole or healthy) but are the usual tokens of the Holy Spirit at work in a life. It's reassuring to know that other people have gone through this and grown and changed and glorified God."

"The sights and sounds of Christmas are beginning. I am like the shepherds—'The glory of the Lord shone round about them and they were sore afraid.' Being sore afraid is the only appropriate human reaction to the glory of God, but we must go toward it in spite of the fear."

"I believe that God wants to enter each of our lives as fully as he entered Mary's. Not that we're all going to get pregnant, but that the concept of incarnation is to be carried into all of creation, not just in some spiritualized way. God doesn't want a Platonic friendship. He wants to become literally incarnate in each of us. The Eucharist is the epitome of his physical identification with us. How can you become more perfectly a part of someone than by letting yourself be eaten by him?"

ENCOUNTER

I stand beneath a night of stars
And see
As far as I can look

Into infinity.
I kneel at the communion rail
And meet
That very infinite
Come down to me—
His flesh to be part of my flesh,
His blood to flow with mine,
His love come from beyond
Creation's farthest sky
As bread and wine.

† † †

It has not been hard for me to see the infinite Son of God in my finite friend Elizabeth Rooney. The more time I spend with her, the more I recognize the vibrancy of Christ living in this "ordinary saint."

Sometimes it is good to have a human model. Elizabeth is just a few years my senior (I have just reached the "fifty-four and ready for more" stage myself), but in my thinking and behavior I find myself imitating her as she herself imitates Christ. Any human contact modifies, shifts, changes us, not always for good. One of the fruits of this continuing friendship is that I sense myself to be different, better, because of Elizabeth. For me, the possibilities of the Christian life are enlarged because of her. By the gentle persuasion of her own clearly focused life she has nudged me into loving Jesus more deeply, openly, constantly, happily, wholeheartedly.

Wholehearted—that's the word. I have been searching for a precise description of this unique friend. *Enthusiastic* is a word that fits her well; its root speaks of the ardor of an in-Godded human. But even more closely, the words wholesome, healthy, healed, hale, whole—all words with a single source can unreservedly be applied to her. They bring to mind the body full of light because of its single eye, as St. Matthew expressed it. As I see her pulling into one the twin strands of the contemplative and active life (not without struggle), she seems to be finding the secret of holding the inner and outer Elizabeth in a whole, and holy, balance. In her the beauty of spirit and the clarity of disciplined intellect seem to translate freely into decisive actions, firm relationships, lucidly spoken words, imaginative prose and verse. In turn, the voice of God speaks to her through the created universe, the church, other people, literature, and the Bible, informing and shaping her inner growth, worship, and belief.

This dynamic ebb and flow moves me profoundly because of its simplicity and naturalness. Elizabeth Rooney, for all her sensitivity and awareness, seems devoid of unhealthy self-consciousness and hubris. For her, the Christian life has not been a human achievement so much as a fervent response to a divine initiative—the outpouring of Gift and Grace to which she holds up her earthen vessel for filling; or, to change the metaphor, the shining Sun towards which she tilts her mirror. Titus describes the process like this: "When the kindness and love of God our Savior appeared, he saved us, not because of righteous things we had done, but because of his mercy. He saved us through the washing of rebirth and renewal by the Holy Spirit, whom he poured out on us generously through Jesus Christ our Savior, so that, having been justified by his grace, we might become heirs having the hope of eternal life" (Ti 3:4-7).

In her journal Elizabeth supplies a vivid analogy for this divine-human joining: "Today in the Cave parking lot there was a puddle— a muddy, shallow puddle on the blacktop, not more than an inch deep at best and perhaps four feet across. When looked at from a certain angle, it reflected all the tree tops in it, and clouds and sky, all the way to infinity. I think I'm like the puddle—muddy, shallow, insignificant—but, by God's grace, capable of the miracle of reflecting him and, in him, all the wonder of the universe. 'We have this treasure in earthen vessels that the glory may be of God and not of man. . . .'"

Hope, in a muddy flower,
Infinity, caught in a shallow pool,
Eternity, in every passing hour,
And you, Creator God, in every fool.

Courtesy of Dorothy Clarke Wilson.

SEVEN

Evelyn Harris Brand

by Gladys Hunt

NO ONE WHO KNEW EVELYN HARRIS during the first thirty years of her life would have guessed that she would one day be a pioneer in missions, an indomitable figure in the hills of South India. Yet no one who knew her during the last thirty years of her life could imagine her as anything else, so single-minded was her concern for the people of the hills. From "retirement" at age seventy until she died at age ninety-five, this wisp of a woman trekked the hills on her pony spreading the Good News, caring for people few others seemed to love. Evelyn Harris Brand is God's kind of surprise in human history.

I first heard of Evelyn from her son, Dr. Paul Brand, a well-known authority on the rehabilitation of lepers. Later, I read the story of Dr. Brand's amazing achievements in India in a book entitled *Ten Fingers for God*, by Dorothy Clarke Wilson. It told of his success with the surgical reconstruction of limbs impaired by leprosy. No author could tell his story without telling something of his mother, and so I read more about Evelyn Brand. I felt unaccountably drawn to this unusual woman, and shortly after reading the book drove with my husband to the leprosarium in Carville, Louisiana, where Paul Brand was working. Subsequently, I entered into correspondence with Evelyn Brand. She was eighty-five years old when she began writing to me, telling me how she and Jesse

Brand had committed themselves to carry the Gospel to the malaria-ridden hills of the Kolli range. Her letters fairly crackled with the fire of her passion for the hill people and for God. But I am getting ahead of my story, which begins in England in 1879.

Evie, as the family called her, was born ninth among eleven children, only two of whom were boys. Both parents were deeply spiritual, and their commitment to God and to his church was of greatest important in their family life. In the loving environment of this home, the children learned to pray, to care about the needy and the lost, and to know the Bible. Evelyn spent time at her mother's knee, learning the scripture and hearing the story of Jesus' love. She came to trust Christ while still very young, feeling a strange stirring in her own heart as she repeated the Beatitudes to her mother. "Blessed are they who hunger and thirst after righteousness, for they shall be filled." She never forgot the importance of that moment, writing to me years later, "Mother brought me to Christ by that word in Matthew, showing me how desire is the proof of the new life to which Jesus was calling those who were thirsty." She was baptized at age eleven in the Strict Baptist Church of England, where her father was superintendent of a thriving Sunday school for unchurched boys and girls.

Mr. Harris, a prosperous London merchant, provided well for his family. All their needs would be met. Servants did the cooking and scrubbing; maids waited on their personal needs. Mr. Harris educated the girls according to the custom of the Victorian age. Their schooling included the three basic R's, a foreign language, and additional training in the arts. He himself possessed a keen artistic sense and collected various works of art, among which were several paintings, a passion Evelyn later shared.

In this loving, supportive environment Evelyn came to womanhood, greatly influenced by the members of her family, caught in a web of dependencies. She had all she needed and more. She was serious-minded, talented in art, and very beautiful. Not only did she excel at painting, but she often sat as a model for others.

Evelyn painted landscapes, broad vistas, sweeping colors, the changing mood of the sky. She liked what Turner did with sunsets and sunrises and sought to model her own work after his. She put together a small book of her water colors, and her oils were in some demand. Her life was full as she tended to various good works and social obligations befitting her standing in society. She loved pretty clothes and, bedecked in gowns of lace and silks, wearing stylish flounces and feathered hats, she cut an attractive figure. She was not unhappy, only restless as time passed. Life did not seem to be heading anywhere, and she found no adequate outlet for the stream of creativity and energy within her. She was now almost thirty years old.

Evelyn later wrote about her childhood: "My girlhood was a happy one, with no hindrances or shortages of anything that was appreciated by girls of that generation. But it was so often overshadowed by self. Years later I found in my childish hand, written when I was about ten, this verse:

Oh, why are children called such
When higher heights they run
In thought and mind
Than many more experienced one?

Jesse Mann Brand both directly and indirectly changed the shape of Evelyn's life. Evelyn had heard about Jesse when he had gone out to India with the Strict Baptist Mission three years earlier. Now she read a booklet he had written in which he described a survey trip he and a Mr. Morling had made to the Kollis Malai, a range of mountains in South India. So graphic was his description of these inaccessible, malaria-ridden mountains and their people that Evelyn felt that she, too, had climbed over the rocks and through the thick undergrowth. She lived vicariously in such adventures and her interest in missions grew. She began to wonder if she could ever be a missionary.

About this time Evelyn accompanied her sister Florrie on a six-week voyage to Australia. Florrie had married an Australian and was returning to him after a short visit to England. This was the first exciting step in uprooting Evelyn for foreign service. Suddenly life was far from ordinary; she was seeing the world, rushing from one side of the ship to the other with her paints and canvas, trying to capture the beauty she saw on every hand as the ship sailed through the Mediterranean Sea, along the coast of Africa, and around the tip of India. On the return journey a fellow passenger, a missionary, told her about Africa and its need. Sensing a responsive spirit in her, he began recruiting her for missionary service. He sought Evelyn out with such fervor that she began to wonder whether it was a missionary call or interest in the man himself that stirred her response—until he casually mentioned his wife. Hurt and embarrassed by her mistaken emotions, Evelyn decided this was not her call. Still, the idea of going abroad to serve Christ became increasingly appealing. The Evelyn who arrived home in England was a freer, more determined Evelyn than the one who had left.

On her return, she went directly to Keswick, to attend the annual Christian conference held there. Her sisters also attended. When the invitation was given for those who felt called to mission service, Evelyn rose to her feet to indicate her willingness. Even so, she made sure she was standing behind a post so that her sisters could not see her and report her decision to their father before she could summon the courage to tell him. She would probably go to India, she thought, for most of her church's mission work was there. But how could she tell her father?

Then, unexpectedly (the way God often works), Jesse Brand, home on furlough, came to speak at the St. Johns Wood Chapel, to which the Harris family belonged. He described his life in Sendamangalam, a small village on the plains of South India, where open sores, disease, poverty, and starvation were the common lot of thousands. He told of epidemics of plague and cholera, of the pressure to minister that kept him from going to thousands on the mountains of death, as the Kollis Malai were called. Evie drank in the details of India's need.

Later Jesse Brand came to the Harris home for tea. Evelyn had many questions to ask, but something about his male vitality and eagerness intimidated her. He seemed to be staring at her with his black eyes, as though he were addressing everything he said solely to her. She shrank back to the edge of the gathering, leaving her sisters to serve the sandwiches and cakes. Everything about Jesse

Brand—his mustache, his eyes, his tone of voice, his dark good looks—seemed a bit overwhelming. Jesse told of how the people of the hills had begged him to come and settle among them.

From that day on Evelyn knew she must tell her father. It was the hardest thing she had ever done. He seemed to grow older before her eyes. Must she go? Weren't there enough heathen in London to convert? *Haven't I provided you with all you need?* He had wanted to keep her safe from the cruel world and make her *comfortable.* But she was choosing a life of discomfort, turning her back on all he offered. She stood before him, beautifully radiant, so eager to serve God. But he had not walked with God all these years to no avail. He, too, cared about the lost. But to send Evelyn? He delayed his decision by asking a doctor to examine her to determine whether she was fit to work in the tropics. To his disappointment, the doctor pronounced her hearty and able to do what her sheltered life had never allowed.

She was accepted by the Church Mission Board, and her passage was booked on a ship to Bombay. As she dressed for a farewell party in her honor, she wondered if she would ever again wear the satins and laces she had thought so important in her life. In the end, it was Evelyn who wept most bitterly at parting from her family. She had not realized how hard it would be. She could not know that she would never see her father again on earth.

In India at last, Evelyn absorbed the sights, sounds, and smells of a totally different world than the one she had known. Hardest of all was learning Tamil. The Strict Baptist Mission had high standards for language study, and this proved a trial for Evelyn, who found languages a snare. And it was so hot in Madras! The students were awakened before dawn when the temperature would already be in the low nineties. If she rested her hands on the table, a puddle formed from her perspiration. The long-sleeved, full-skirted dresses the missionaries wore were oppressive, and at night, crawling under mosquito netting seemed akin to smothering.

But gradually, she adjusted to both the study and the heat, and later began making visits in the city with the Bible women. Then young Jesse Brand appeared in Madras. His appointment had been to Sendamangalam, which was several hundred miles to the

Southwest. Now he was to take over the work in Madras. Evelyn wondered how she could ever have been intimidated by him; he was so fun-loving and attractive. One day he said to her, "I knew you'd be coming. I could see it on your face when I spoke about the hill people."

Evelyn's fascination with the hill people drew them together. He helped her with language study, and they began to share plans and dreams, discovering a common love for nature and for beauty and a deep dedication to God. When Evie went to Coonoor in the Nilgiri Hills, Jesse began courting her by mail. His plans for medical study were changing, he said. He was requesting that the Mission Board allow him to begin work in the hills as soon as the Booths returned from furlough. His letters contained endearments and, at last, a proposal for marriage. Evelyn and Jesse were deeply in love.

Mrs. Elnaugh, the widow who was to accompany Evelyn to the hills, became ill and had to return to England. Now, in the incredible way God works in human lives, she would go with Jesse. "I would gladly have gone alone," she said, "but with Jesse! Where could one get closer to heaven!" Only these two felt such a strong call to the hill people.

Suddenly Evie became desperately ill with typhoid. For days she was delirious with fever and pain. Just as she was on the point of undertaking what seemed her life's work, she was struck down by illness. Would her hopes end in ruin? The answer came—a definite no. With the help of friends she was nursed back to health and recovered her strength.

Meanwhile, Jesse had been up in the hills building their simple house, which he had framed on the plains in Sendamangalam. Coolies had carried the house in sections up the tortuous paths to the hilltop where Jesse and Evelyn would begin life together in "the mountains of death." It was the same house from which she wrote to me fifty years later.

Evelyn never tired of telling the story of their wedding day, recounting the events with amusement and nostalgia. It was August 1913. The chapel in Sendamangalam was packed with the grateful patients of Jesse Brand, who had done medical work among them. Evelyn was amazed and humbled by their love for Jesse, which was now showered on her as garland after garland was placed around her neck. She was so weighed down that she had to take one lot off to make way for the second. Here at Senda-mangalam she saw the hills for the first time, misty blue against the sky. She and Jesse planned to spend their honeymoon in their new home on the hills.

Wedding dress and all, they rode the first rough five miles in a jutkka cart to the foot of the Kollis Hills. Jesse had arranged for bearers to meet them and carry the two of them in dholies to their home. He had said it would be a real wedding procession. It was late afternoon when they approached the base of the hill. The dholies were there, but the coolies were missing. They had gone off on a pig hunt, said the anxious sahib who helped make the arrangements. While Evelyn sat on the jungle path guarding the baggage, Jesse and the sahib rushed off to find other bearers. Thunder sounded in the distant sky, and monsoon clouds gathered.

Jesse returned with four bearers for Evelyn and enough men to carry the baggage. Sitting on the dholie—a rough hammock of canvas fastened to bamboo poles—with her wedding dress tucked over her knees, Evelyn clung to the bamboo poles. Eager to get up the steep paths before dark, the coolies began to jog along. The rolling motion and the heat gave her a wilted, sick feeling. The paths became steeper and thorns tore at her dress. Then the clouds opened and the rain came, transforming the dholie into a veritable bath tub. She sat there rocking along in sodden grace.

"Are you all right?" Jesse asked worriedly. This was not the wedding night he had so carefully planned.

"Fine," said Evelyn. "I was needing a bath."

They laughed together, both aware that they would need their sense of humor often in adjusting to this life. They finally arrived, both of them mud-streaked and soaked to the skin.

Well, thought Evelyn, this is not going to be easy, and I might just as well know it now. Later, Jesse presented her with their prayer book, entitled *Evie's and My Prayer Book*. It is her most precious memory of that eventful day. One column was for prayer requests, the other for praise when the prayers were answered. It was the first of many such books they would keep as a witness to God's faithfulness to them.

Engraved inside Evelyn's wedding band are the words *Trust and Triumph*. Jesse Brand had taken courage from these words on a wall motto when Evelyn's life was threatened by typhoid fever in Coonoor. In their new home, Evelyn made her own wall motto with those words, forming them out of eucalyptus leaves, and fastening them to a board. For the next sixty years those words directed her life. At eighty-nine she made them the title of a small autobiography she wrote.

Jesse Mann Brand was a gifted man, if not a genius. He was a clever builder, making their home not only weathertight, but enjoyably liveable in its simple fashion. He taught young men in the villages to build, and the results of his skill dot the mountains of South India. He built huts, schools, dispensaries, and chapels to meet the needs of the various stations he and Evelyn established. Before leaving England he had taken a missionary medical course at Livingston College, and had an intuitive sense for diagnosing and treating illnesses. His strategy for reaching the hill people included opening schools, teaching trades, instructing people in basic hygiene, cleaning their wells, and introducing new agricultural techniques and products. As time went on he taught the people to make tiles to replace the thatch on the roofs, which provided breeding places for rats and vermin and which frequently went up in smoke from the torches people carried at night. He planted orange trees and sugar cane and taught the people how to market them. He raised poultry and sheep. Both he and Evelyn had a resourcefulness and determination that equipped them for this work.

Evelyn wrote about him, "Jesse seemed made for the hills." He not only had the vision, but the energy to carry out his plans. He was a teacher, preacher, naturalist, and scholar. Evie constantly marvelled at this man she had married. In his spare time he read books like Carlyle's *French Revolution*, Bunyan's *Grace Abounding*, and books on relativity and mathematics. Evelyn once commented on the folly of the struggle to gain knowledge when death would only cut it all short.

Jesse responded, "Why, you infidel, this is only the beginning. I think of Heaven as going on to learn and know that after which we can seek but feebly here!"

Nothing about the hills made for an easy mission field. To say that the terrain was rugged is a monstrous understatement. The people were animistic, caught in the worship of devils. They had a "pig cult"—not worshipping the pig, but pouring out the blood as a libation to Karapen, the head of devils. The witch doctor or priest (the *poosari*) was greatly feared, and his word had great authority, especially in the matter of illness. Without education and contact with the outside world, the people lived in fear, bound by caste. Few government officials ever spent the night on the hills, even though bungalows were provided for the forestry department. They feared contracting malaria, the deadly plague of the mountains. To make matters worse, bears, leopards, and other wild beasts made travel dangerous.

Evelyn tells a bear story that happened early in their stay in the Kollis. A bear attacked a woman as she and her husband walked through the jungle. The man ran to her rescue, and the bear turned on him, felling him with one blow. The man would have been killed had not his tiny, timid, pregnant wife kept pushing at the bear until it ran off. The man was brought to the Brands the next day. Jesse stitched for hours, closing the torn scalp and leg and setting the arm. The man stayed on for further treatments, and they were able to tell him the Gospel again and again. They had not yet built a place for in-patients to stay, and took advantage of the poosari's offer to house their patient in his grain shed. It seemed generous of him until they realized that the poosari had frightened the man, threatening him not to listen to the white man's religion.

But the man recovered and spread Jesse's fame as a doctor throughout the villages. People began coming from all over the Kollis. In one year the Brands treated 1,500 patients.

Evelyn and Jesse went on extensive camping trips to reach

people across the Kollis range. Everywhere they went, crowds gathered for medical help and heard the Good News. While Jesse treated the sick, Evie would teach the women about clean water and mosquito nets or other needs she saw in their lives. When Jesse preached, eager crowds gathered to hear. Their hopes would rise as they answered inquirers. But, in the end, no one was willing to break caste and become a Christian.

Evelyn wrote to Mrs. Booth in Madras, asking her to send a lady's sidesaddle, for she was expecting a baby. Mrs. Booth was aghast that she would travel those "wild hills" on a horse when she was pregnant. She did go down to Ooctacamond, about a hundred miles away, when the time for delivery came. On July 17, 1914, Evelyn Harris Brand, age thirty-five, gave birth to Paul Wilson Brand, who was promptly dedicated to God's service. It was a gruelling business to have a baby so far from home. Getting back up the hills with a baby meant first a carriage ride, then the train, then bullock cart, and finally the dholie up the rough, steep terrain. But she was home at last, and her beautiful baby boy gave her many more opportunities to minister to the women. Two years later, a daughter, Connie, was born into the family. Both children accompanied them on the camping trips across the Kollis Range.

As the years went on, Jesse and Evie became increasingly incensed at the evil ways of the hill people. It was common practice to marry small children to adults in order to get more farm workers. A mature girl might be married to a small boy so that the father could have an extra worker. Then she would be forced to bear children for his use by any man available. This man would be a "kept man" and also work the land. Immorality and venereal disease were widespread, and it was the women who suffered most. Evie's solution was to get the children into schools, to teach them the joy of study. It was only then that they would be able to resist early marriages, she reasoned.

Still no converts came. The poosaris kept the people away. They knew what belief in the Yesu-Swami would do to their own power over the people. "Believe in the Yesu-Swami if you choose," they said, "but you must worship the other swamis, too."

It was 1919, the year of the worldwide influenza epidemic.

People were baffled by this unknown illness, and there were no sulfa drugs to help fight the epidemic. The hill people simply fled from each other, rather than trying to deal with it. Left to die alone, the sick struggled and succumbed with no one to feed them or give them so much as a drink of water. Jesse and Evie took around rice gruel to keep the people from dehydration. Even so the death rate was high. The poosari was frightened and would not even take part in the funerals.

Then one day news came that the poosari and his family were sick. Evelyn ran to their compound and found the wife in the middle of the court, clinging to a string cot, struggling for breath. The poosari lay on the mud verandah of his swami-hut, panting with pneumonia. On the verandah of their own home, crying by herself, lay their unfed nine-month-old baby girl. Evie offered them hot rice gruel, but the poosari had lost all hope. "You must take our baby," he gasped. "Don't give it to the village people. If God lets me live, I will come to the bungalow to worship Jesus."

The poosari and his wife died shortly thereafter, the poosari calling on the name of Jesus. Jesse and Evelyn named the little girl Ruth, for long ago Ruth left her kindred to join the people of God. This was the breakthrough for which they had prayed, and it came from an unexpected quarter.

They continued camping, treating the sick, building schools, facing disappointments, and embracing new hope. While they were camping in the hills, Ruth's brother came and brought another boy with him. Both of them wanted to live with the Brands. Later a boy with a chronic face ulcer got permission from his grandfather to join them. They were now feeding and clothing four children besides their own. Eventually they sent the boys to be educated in a Brethren School for Boys. Years later those boys were among those the mission sent to work with their people in the hills.

Another triumph came when a hill man, Solomon, joined them, despite the threats of his poosari. He boldly announced he was leaving his old ways and following the Yesu-Swami. He brought his reluctant wife, who later also became a believer. His father, David, joined him in the faith. The door was swinging open.

Jesse and Evelyn taught their own children in lieu of formal schooling. What an exciting pair they were! Jesse fed the children's curiosity about nature, telling them stories, taking apart a white ant's tower, examining insects or whatever came into their path. Evelyn carried her canvas and boards in a knapsack, and while she was painting would teach the children to notice the world around them. "Look at the sky! How can I capture those colors?" She let Paul do his arithmetic up in his favorite tree, dropping his finished paper to his mother, who sat below. They would soon return to England on furlough. In accordance with mission rules they would have to leave the children behind when they returned to India. Both parents were determined to make the most of every minute spent with their children.

From the outset, the children shared their parents' concerns for the hill people. They did their best to teach baby Ruth. "Mother, we are teaching her that she must leave her old swamis and pray to Jesus." Returning home after visiting in several villages, Paul wanted to stop at yet another village. Evelyn protested that she was too tired. Paul said, "But, Mummy, we must or they will go on worshipping their false gods."

They prayed together about the problems in the work, about their joys and sorrows. Evelyn said, "We did not teach our children how to pray. We simply included them in our prayers from their earliest years." Later, separated from the children, their letters kept those close ties alive. Jesse wrote to Paul: "Yesterday when I was riding over the wind-swept hilltops around Kulivalavu, I could not help thinking of an old hymn that begins 'Heaven above is deeper blue, flowers with purer beauty glow.' When I am alone on these long rides, I just love the sweet-smelling world, the dear brown earth, the lichen on the rocks, the heaps of dead brown leaves drifted like snow in the hollows. God means us to delight in his world. Just observe. Remember. Compare. And be always looking to God with thankfulness and worship for having placed you in such a delightful corner of the universe as Planet Earth."

The work kept growing. Teachers and preachers came from the plains to staff the schools. Five stations were open with schools and chapels. Jesse used hill men to build, teaching them to be sawyers and carpenters. Those who became Christians were often forced out of their own villages and came to live near the Brand's compound, making it a strong Christian settlement.

By 1923 they had spent ten years on the hills. It was time to leave for a year. A year too late for Evelyn to see her father. A letter had come saying that he had collapsed while leading his beloved Sunday school and had never regained consciousness. When Evelyn told the children, "We're going home," they looked at her in wonder. "But this is home, Mummy." It was all they knew. Nevertheless they were going for their first journey out—home to England.

Evelyn's culture shock at England was as great as her children's. Rooms full of furniture, fancy clothes, wearing gloves to church, and shoes! It seemed a confining world. Damask, fine china, and silver, for two uninhibited small creatures from the jungle, took some getting used to. The long, polished balustrade was an irresistible slide. The family invaded the placid life of Evelyn's two unmarried sisters, who cared for their elderly mother, and who would care for Paul and Connie when they returned to India.

Jesse was away in the churches, reporting on the work in the hills. It was a good year, and it passed all too quickly. The children were enrolled in schools, and it was time to leave them behind. Paul and Connie were to recite five Tamil Bible verses every Sunday morning at breakfast. Evie painted other texts by their beds. . . . *I will be a father unto you. . . . As one whom a mother comforteth, so I will comfort you.* Leaving them behind was the greatest test of loyalty she ever had to face.

A month later Jesse and Evelyn were back at their little settlement. An eager crowd greeted them with music and garlands. They were home. *Stottherum, stottherum*—Praise, praise. These words were more and more on Evie's lips.

Jesse had collected money in England for a girls' home, and he set about to build it. Little Ruth came back to be with them. Word soon spread over the hills that there was a place for unwanted children. Because of the practice of marrying children at an early age, an unwanted child-wife might later be evicted. One after another of these children came to the Brands. Babies left to die on rubbish heaps were brought to Evie. Some did not live, but she loved and cared for them as they came to her home until the girls' home was finished in 1925. This home grew to twenty girls, ranging from infants to adolescents. They were given an elementary education by a Tamil teacher from the plains. Many of them became Christians. When they were older, marriages were arranged for them with young Christian men. "The first sound of every day in the Settlement, as dawn is breaking, is a song of praise from the girls in the Home," Jesse wrote in a report to the churches back home.

A small boys' hostel was also begun. A Mission Industrial School taught both boys and girls practical skills. Jesse planted two acres with mulberry bushes and bought silk worms. He discovered what government aid was available for the hill people in order to receive help for his projects. Dr. Samuel, a Syrian Christian from the ancient church in Travancore, came to work with them. The fact that the government paid his salary is a comment on their esteem for the work the Brands were doing.

Sometimes Evelyn traveled with Jesse to the plains when he was asked to speak. He wrote to the children on the occasion of one train journey, "Mother nearly frantic because she could not paint both sides at once."

The work was becoming more demanding. Jesse was preaching in over ninety hamlets surrounding their six stations. Over 25,000 people were given medical attention in a year's time. He spent hours reading law books to obtain rights for the hill people. He took a band of simply clad men from the hills to a government office to protest their exploitation by landlords living on the plains and got rulings that prohibited ownership of hill land by absentee landlords. He formed a cooperative society at a bank so that farmers would not need to pay ruinous 35% interest rates to moneylenders on the plains.

One day, in 1928, Jesse stood with Evie on a high crest near one of their stations. They looked beyond the Kollis to the horizon where, ranged in stark grandeur and mystery, stood four other mountain ranges—the Pachais, the Kalyrans, and beyond them, the Peria Malai and the Chitteris. "We must go to them," said Jesse, "to all five of them. Before we die we must go to all five ranges and take the saving message of Jesus Christ." It was a vision they shared, a commitment they made together.

By 1928 the Christian community in the settlement on the Kollis had grown to fifty. There were nine schools on the Kollis. The mission farm was feeding the whole community. The carpenter shop and the silk industry were thriving. The Brands were due for furlough in 1929, but, as had happened before, another missionary family seemed to need it more, so they agreed to postpone it for a year. "It will pass quickly," Jesse said cheerfully to Evelyn, who was thinking of the children. "Who knows? This one year may bring the greatest blessing of all."

The mission was facing difficulties and Jesse was asked to visit the churches of South India. He was gone for two months. He returned more tired than Evelyn had ever seen him, yet even more full of hope. When he complained of a fever, his temperature at 106, the doctor thought it was malaria. Never having seen blackwater fever, both the doctor and Evie were slow to realize what was happening. In the tortuous days and nights that followed, Evie listened to her beloved Jesse calling for water he could not possibly retain, saw his flesh turn dry and yellow, his eyes glaze, and his blood drain away. Now it was too late to take him out of the hills to a hospital. It was unbelievable. Four days later, on June 15, Jesse Brand died of blackwater fever at age forty-four. Evelyn was too dazed to respond.

In a letter written to me when she was eighty-five, she was still asking herself why she had not taken Jesse away for a rest. Why hadn't she known it was so serious? She said, "As I write this I have just asked my Indian co-worker Paul Chakkaravathy these questions and he answered me, 'Did you not teach me that our Lord said that one sparrow does not fall to the ground without the Father seeing it, and cannot you see that it was all according to God's will?' God is the first and the last. He never makes a mistake."

Evelyn did what needed doing. She said the right words and encouraged the community, saw to it that the funeral service focused on Christian hope, but she felt dead inside. The Mission Board expected her to leave at once, but she stayed on, stubbornly refusing to leave.

Evelyn had one resolve: to see that the work in the hills continued. She must save the work for which Jesse gave his life. The Mission Board had never given it more than half-hearted support. She would wait until someone else was appointed. She was bewildered at this terrible sweeping break in their plans to reach the hills. Writing to me about Jesse's death she enclosed this poem, and the pain in her letter seemed as fresh as it might have been thirty-five years earlier:

We were only one
So when the sun shone,
Shone on us,
It shone on one.

And when the rain came
It was just the same
It rained on one
It fell on one.

When He withheld from us
'Twas ever thus,
We were but one
To feel the miss
Of any bliss
Under the sun.

Then came the storm
The cold and bitter weather.
It hurt us not,
For we were one together.

When He took him away
Nothing was left
But a heart bereft
With no one to share
No one to care.

No, He who took him is here,
No one by my side,
But He is my guide.

One day in her misery she set out on a lonely trek riding Jesse's horse. She had never ridden this high-spirited animal, preferring her own plodding mare. She seemed to have lost all fear, thinking it would be better to die than to face life alone. On her way to a distant village she remembered that Jesse had told her just before his death that he had found a new way, a path that avoided the steep outcropping of rocks that made the way a narrow ledge. She had always been frightened on this path, even when Jesse was with her. Now, she thought, I will never find it. Suddenly Jesse's horse turned at a right angle and entered into the jungle bushes and trees. She gave it rein. Hardly breathing, she sat quietly while the horse crossed a stream and went through the woods, arriving at the village. Tears blurred her vision as these words came to her, "I will bring the blind by a way they know not; I will lead them in paths they have not known. These things I will do unto them and not forsake them." (Is 42:16) It was a promise from God for the future.

Before long, Evelyn decided that it was time to return to England on furlough. She seemed suspended between two worlds when she arrived in England to find Paul a boy of fifteen and Connie thirteen. Her arms were starved for these precious children she had so reluctantly left behind a few years earlier. Connie with the same golden hair, and Paul, a reserved, self-conscious young man. Connie flew into her arms, sobbing. Paul was more remote, almost in shock.

Years later he told me his reaction to that meeting. He was almost giddy with excitement on the way to the boat. He pictured his mother as she had been when he last saw her—tall, beautiful, vibrantly alive. Instead he saw this unbelievably shrunken, *little*, old lady coming down the gangplank. He had to keep telling himself, "This is my mother!" He felt torn with grief over his father's death—and now this reality of what his father's death had done to his beautiful mother. He couldn't believe it was true.

In the year that she remained in England, Evie encouraged her children, particularly Paul, to become missionaries. Both have done so. Through all their separations they remained close, united in their concern to spread the Good News. Evelyn wrote in a letter to me, "No earthly relationship can be like the one where mother and child meet at the footstool of the same Lord."

Evie knew she must return to India. Her commitment was to God and, although she might be less than half a person, she knew that even a broken vessel can carry living water. The Mission Board refused to return her to the Kollis Malai. It was not sound policy, they said. But her arguments were persuasive. She had helped create the work on the Kollis, and she wanted to return. They had built most of the work with their own hands—she and Jesse—and with their own money which she received in a trust from her father. Finally it was agreed that she could go to the Kollis. She sailed in the autumn of 1930. Feeling fearfully alone and weak, she expressed herself in a poem.

And must I now go on alone with You,
And is there no one near to hold my hand?
And no one who can really understand?
"I'll do it all for you."
But there'll be silence round me all the time,
Silence which even You with all your infinite resource
Cannot break through.

"Silence to hear My voice, that's all,
And I have planned it all for you.
You have been speaking all the time,
You would not listen, now no other choice
But to sit still and hear My voice."

Speak, Lord, thy servant waits to hear
Thy gentle whisper, strong and clear.

The hill people came from all over the Kollis, bearing gifts and garlands of flowers. Their Mother had come home. She ploughed into the work—loving, teaching, exhorting, feeding on the beauty of the hills. But this five-year term on the Kollis for which she had fought was filled with tension and frustration. First one couple and then another were in charge of the work, and none of them had Jesse's gifts. She had been co-creator and co-manager of the work for over sixteen years, and now she was under the authority of others who did not understand the people as she did—and who made policies she did not approve. She didn't hesitate to speak out. And it couldn't have been easy for other dedicated missionaries to see their predecessor honored and sought after while they were bypassed. The people called her *Mother* or *Honored Lady.*

She knew she must give these hills to others. But what of the other mountain ranges they claimed for God? Perhaps she should go to the Pachais where she and Jesse had already camped. Or to the Kalyrans?

Her mind was busy with all kinds of ideas. She even drew plans for a house, with a dispensary attached. But her mission refused to consider it. The leaders even questioned the value of work on the Kollis. She wrote to Connie: "Do you know, Con, I feel like a mother with a baby, and when you see a crowd of people seize it, feel its pulse, shake it a bit . . . and discuss whether it should live or die!" She was hot in her protest.

Again in 1936 she went home to England for a furlough. She cared little for clothes or fashion—she who had once been so conscious of lace and frills. Even though her sisters badgered her about her wardrobe, she would pick an unbecoming dress, hopelessly outmoded. Her disregard for the amenities of life were more and more part of their non-conformist sister. But when she spoke, she held her audience spellbound. She was radiant with love for the Lord.

She returned to India in 1937, assigned to work on the plains in Sendamangalam—she who loved the hills. At least she was in sight of them here, and whenever she could, she went up to the mountains to camp. She returned to the Peria Malai, believing it offered the best possibilities for developing a work. She searched the hills for a good place to begin, but the mission frowned on her interest and sent her to Madras. It was like leaving the promised land to go back into the wilderness for three years.

Almost ten years had passed since she was in England, and the war was over. When she arrived home again in England, Paul noticed, to his surprise, that she did not really seem to age after fifty-five. She was frail-looking, her features pared to the bone. She wore her grey hair short, straight, and tied with a ribbon. Her eyes were young and piercing. She met David Wilmshurst and Connie's baby Jessica, and Paul's wife Margaret and their two-year-old Christopher. For the first time she was called Granny, somewhat to her dismay. From that day on people everywhere began referring to her as Granny Brand, a name she never really agreed to.

She was now near retirement age. The board suggested she stay in England. She was getting *too old for the work*, they said. She seethed at that remark—she who had gone up the mountains, lain in her mosquito net hut through drenching rains, traveled on horseback from village to village. She begged the mission to send her back to India for one year. Reluctantly they yielded to her request. But Granny Brand had a plan. She would give the mission the required year in Sendamangalam and then she would retire—in India. She would take the Gospel to the next of the five ranges as she and Jesse had planned to do. The Kollis had come first. She would go the Kalyrans, then the Pachais. The income from her father would support her work.

And that is exactly what Evelyn Brand did. Up until now her story may be no more or less remarkable than that of many missionaries of her caliber. At seventy she began to finish what she and Jesse had begun. She had arranged for a mud hut with a thatched roof to be built for her. Up the mountains she went, with a small caravan of coolies carrying her goods. Later two retired Indian workers came to live with her and, for a time, her daughter Ruth and Ruth's husband, John Michael.

As in the Kollis, the people came flocking to her for medical help, and she ferreted out those who did not come. She battled epidemics of typhoid, dengue, and even cholera. She delivered babies and fought malnutrition. A procession of adopted children came into her life, children who needed education to serve God.

On the way down hill in a dholi one day Evelyn was careless, neglecting to hold firmly to the side poles. When one of the bearers fell, Evelyn pitched forward and hit her head on a rock. The pain was almost intolerable, but she had to travel miles further by dholi, then by bus, then a train ride of a hundred miles and then another crowded bus. She was in a daze when she arrived at the hospital. The doctors treated her and took X-rays of her injured spine, but did not discover the seriousness of the fall. She never completely recovered from that fall, and her feet were partially paralyzed from then on.

Walking became difficult. Back in the village sometime later she tripped over the doorway and broke her leg. After that she needed to wear special shoes with braces, and walked with two unmatched bamboo sticks—a terrible nuisance, she said. But at least she could still ride a horse. Over the next years, fifteen workers came to help in the mountains, and only two stayed.

The work began growing in the Kalyrans. A few hill people became Christians. Evie worked four different stations. Following Jesse's model she cleared land and consulted with the government horticulturists to find supplements for the diet of the villagers. Schools were established, and the government agreed to pay the teacher's salaries if she would find the teachers. She paid for much of the school land from her own meager income. She had a nose for sin on the one hand, and a trusting spirit—to the point of gullibility—on the other. She was cheated and bilked out of money and property by people who saw she was careless in keeping accounts.

Paul despaired of the way his mother gave things away. Once he visited her and brought two dozen blankets. On his next visit she scarcely had one for herself. Connie chided her and said it was wrong to give so much away. Granny's comment: "Well, I'm glad the Lord hasn't shown *me* it's wrong."

Three young women under the New Tribes Mission started a station on the Chitteris range and worked in cooperation with the Hill Gospel Fellowship. Three of the five ranges now had a witness. Only two more to go, thought Evie. She was taking on more workers for the hills.

When Evelyn was eighty-five, Paul made one of his treks to find her. He climbed for hours, rigorous climbing that left him exhausted. He talked at length about the work, telling her how much had been accomplished, how well the work was going in the Kalyrans. It was time to leave now, he said. Granny agreed. It *was* time to leave, so she packed up and headed for the Pachais, her third mountain range. Here in a crude hut, with the same opposition, the same need, the hundreds of miles over stony trails, camping out in all kinds of weather, she began again.

When Granny wrote letters, she used a wretched old typewriter that evidently didn't secure the lines. And often in her haste she typed over the previous line, making it an "adventure-in-under-standing" to read her letters. When someone offered to type her letter to me, she refused and wrote, "It's all true. I've been careless not putting full stops, etc., sending disgraceful letters everywhere—people not able to read, etc., but . . ." She assumed I knew the people about whom she wrote and her letters were full of half-stories and allusions. She preached to me, wanting to make certain the college students with whom I worked truly were converted to Christ, that I wasn't just polishing the dirt off, as she said.

"It's terribly marvelous to be used by God," she wrote. For those who were worried about her walking over such rough terrain she wrote, "I can wobble along with my canes, but this is my text, 'Thou hast beset me behind and before, and laid thine hand upon me.' That's a great Psalm to learn by heart. . . . The all-enclosing power of God."

Later she wrote, "I am more conscious of failure than success and see the need for confessions more than congratulations."

No one worked in the hills if they were afraid of sacrifice. Granny herself was a tough reed. She seemed immune to illness, riding across the hills on her pony and entering squalid huts to treat fearful diseases. When she tired, she tethered her pony in a beautiful spot, took off the saddle and used it for a pillow. On one occasion she was advised not to come to a meeting of the Hill Fellowship because monsoon rains made the paths too slippery for her horse. The steady downpour continued and the group couldn't believe she would come. Yet, knowing her, they were hesitant to begin without her. Just then a postal runner arrived with the news that Evie had reached the last and largest river, which was swollen with waters up to a man's armpits, and the bearers of her dholi had refused to go further.

Just as they were leaving to investigate how she was faring, along came four men bearing a dholi at a rapid trot, a tiny figure on board, dripping muddy water. *How?* they asked. It was simple, she said. Taking off her shoes and braces, she had crawled to the edge of the rushing stream, grabbed hold of the rope that went across the river and let herself into the river. Seeing this, the bearers rushed to her aid and carried her across because her legs got tangled up in her ballooning skirt. She'd just have a small wash and a change of clothes and they could get on with the meeting.

In addition to the five ranges she and Jesse claimed for God, she discovered the Gothais and the Paithur Hills. By 1967 Granny was working on all seven ranges. That year she made fourteen trips up and down on horse or in a dholi.

For years Evelyn had hoped to find a doctor who felt called to the hills. Whenever she spoke at the Vellore Medical College, she gave the challenge. Now a young man, Dr. David Lister, a descendant of the great Sir Joseph Lister, heard that call. In Granny he recognized a quality of selfless dedication akin to his own. "She was happier and more alive than anyone I had ever met," he said. "When she looks at you, it's as if she could see right through you."

When she was ninety-five, her frail body seemed to be kept active only by the intensity of her inner zeal. She could scarcely rise to a standing position without help, especially since her favorite sitting place was on the floor.

In the fall of 1974, hearing of an adulterous relationship between two hill people on the Kollis, she went up to her wooden bungalow in the settlement to help solve the issue. There, on her way to chapel, she fell and gashed her head on the corner of the house, but still she insisted on speaking. From the Kollis, she went to the Kalyrans. Granny sent message after message to backsliding Christians, exhorting and forgiving.

She was excited that Paul would be visiting in October in Vellore, and then impatient to get back to the hills in November. Then she fell again. "The Sands of Time are sinking fast," said

Granny, and repeated most of the sixteen stanzas of that hymn. Her speech became jumbled, but she remained strong otherwise. Her pulse, which had been an irregular forty, now became a regular eighty, as if she were climbing that last Summit. On December 18, 1974, she gave one deep sigh and went to heaven.

The next morning a thanksgiving service was held in the Vellore Hospital Chapel. Then a procession began up the Kolli Malai, where in the chapel Jesse built sixty years before, the sorrowful community paid tribute to her. Late that afternoon she was laid to rest beside Jesse Mann Brand. She had written:

You'll say it's a dream that must come true
For the promise is sure to me and to you
That the seed that is sown and watered with tears
Must produce a harvest in after years.

For Evelyn Harris Brand, it proved to be *Trust and Triumph*.

Sources

In telling Evelyn Brand's story, I have relied heavily on the careful research of Dorothy Clarke Wilson and her exciting full-length book, *Granny Brand* (Christian Herald Books: Chappaqua, N.Y., 1976). Regrettably, this is no longer in print.

Evelyn Brand's autobiography, *Trust and Triumph,* published by the International Gospel League, 854 East Washington Boulevard, Pasadena, California 91102, gives colorful insights into her life and the lives of the hill people.

I am also indebted to Dr. Howard T. Lewis of the International Gospel League for his help in getting materials to me—and beyond that, for his vision for Granny Brand's work and for taking on the funding of these needy projects in India.

And last, but surely not least, I want to thank Dr. Paul and Dr. Margaret Brand for sharing so much information and for letting me know Granny through them.

EIGHT

Wilma Burton

by Karen Burton Mains

MY MOTHER DIED UNEXPECTEDLY at her winter residence in Florida. The phone call came from far away bearing the terrible news. My brother-in-law's voice. The awful words.

"Lord . . . Lord . . ." I prayed, then remembered. *Today is my birthday.*

This year I will turn forty on the first anniversary of my mother's death.

First anniversaries after any death are hard. I remember the first Christmas, the first baby born, the first wedding day after my father died. What is missing, what is absent, what is so wounding? Where are the bouyant, familiar sounds? The grand words? The deep pride in family? The laughter? The hilarity? The serious, intense discussions?

Naturally, I am wary about marking this midlife date, cautious about this coming junction of birth and death.

We have always measured our births by decades—Gram, my mother, myself, my son. Mother was a firstborn child, as was I, as is he. My grandmother was twenty when her first, a daughter, was born. Mother was thirty at my birth. I turned twenty in the hospital. In fact, mother was forty at the birth of my brother.

151

So by this arithmetic, we counted our days. Randall, my son, will be twenty. Craig, my brother, will be thirty. Mother would have been seventy. Gram will be ninety. I will turn forty on the first anniversary of my mother's death.

As a child, poking through bureau drawers, I found a letter, sealed and hidden beneath the paper lining. It was addressed: "To Dick." My father. Lacking propriety like most young, I opened it. Mother's handwriting is tight and small, without bold loops and slashes. The letter was to have been read posthumously, in case of death at childbirth.

The letter is gone now. I have not found it in the sorting we have done after death. The remains—such a euphemism; the remains are not the body from which breath and warmth have fled. The remains are the contents of drawers and files and cupboards and closets.

We made three lists. One for myself. One for Valerie, my sister, and one for Craig. Valerie will take the Roseville vase. I will take the blue and white china cannister set. The maple bedroom furniture goes to Craig. This jewelry to mother's close friends. These boxes for the garage sale. This pile of junk is to be thrown into the dumpster.

We are also the remains, we three. We remain.

One finds old pictures and thinks, "Mother must have been my age. Craig was just a baby." In my heart, I beg secret forgiveness for being the eldest child with the longest memory and not knowing how young, how lovely Mother was at forty.

We remain . . . and soon I will turn forty, and in the middle of this fresh and early grief I must understand the meaning of my mother's life and the essence of it for me.

Doctors told my mother, Wilma Inez Wicklund Burton, not to have children. Rheumatic fever had bedridden her for a year in her early twenties, threatening her life. She survived but with damage to the valves of her heart.

One fiancee had been tall and slender, dark with wavy hair, a literature major and a student of Shakespeare. I can hear mother repeating to me his long-ago words, "Well, it's every man's right to have children." The wedding was cancelled.

One of life's many ironies is that mother, who the doctors said should never have children, gave birth to three, while he, a man I never met whose picture is in the boxes in the attic, never had any.

Wilfred Burton, "Dick" to his aunts and uncles who raised him and nicknamed him after the death of his own mother, on the other hand, was not reluctant at all about Wilma Wicklund.

"I want you all to meet the woman I'm going to marry," he announced at a gathering of the Burton clan.

Mother was stupefied. She protested the rain of congratulations. I can see her in my mind's eye, flustered, her peach complexion blushing. They had never talked about marriage. She had only known this man a short time. She was not at all sure, recovering from a broken engagement, that this was the man *she* wanted to marry.

My father-to-be was a music professor, slightly balding and short of stature. (I can remember him saying once with surprise in his eyes, "All my life, on the inside, I've *felt* like a big man, like a tall man.") The possibility that this woman he loved might never be able to have children seemed not to have phased him at all.

I know *I* would have preferred the forthright music teacher to the literary aesthete. It is wonderful to be wanted, to be really wanted.

So mother wrote a letter to the man who loved her enough to risk birth. It was to be read in case her heart failed, in case she died in labor. "To Dick," her tight handwriting scribled. And I, a child, found it unopened and split the seal because I was so much a part of my mother I never dreamed she would hold any secrets from me, her firstborn. And I discovered, what weight this knowledge, that she had risked death at my birth.

Her heart did fail on my birthday—thirty-nine years later, two-and-a-half years after my father's death. My parents, though eternal now, are probably still surprised by this chronicle of earthly events. I think they expected another order in dying.

People often ask me, "How did you start writing?" My answer has always been, "I have this mother who never said to me, 'How are you doing?' but always asked, 'What are you writing?'"

Most certainly, it was mother who, more than any other,

influenced my earliest attempts at writing. She gave me the love of the rhythm of words. She identified my innate ability. She encouraged me to enter writing contests. She planted in my heart the knowledge that reading is wonderful.

Wilma Burton was a published and prize-winning poet. During her life she belonged to many professional writer's organizations like The Poets Club of Chicago, The Chicago Poets and Patrons, and especially The National League of American Pen Women, whose magazine, *The Pen Woman*, she edited for many years, beginning in 1974.

Numerous honors came in tribute to her skills as a teacher at writers' conferences in more than half a dozen states, as an award-winning contestant herself and a judge in poetry contests, and as a writer of four books: *I Need a Miracle Today, Lord*; *Sidewalk Psalms and Some from Country Lanes*; *Without a Man in the House*; and *Living Without Fear*.

In July of 1981, at the Fifth World Congress of Poets in San Francisco, the World Academy of Arts and Culture of Taipei, Republic of China, awarded my mother an honorary doctorate of literature for her contributions to world poetry.

Perhaps most intriguing of all, these accomplishments all happened after Mother was forty, the majority taking place in her fifth and sixth decade. In addition, her books were written and published during a period of tortuous duress, the four years of my father's institutionalization after he suffered brain damage due to encephalitis, and in the two years of grief immediately following his death.

She wrote a poem a day; poems were her prayer language. She rose early—4:00 or 4:30 A.M., as do I. The phone call that came at 6:00 A.M. was invariably from mother. In those fresh hours she gave expression to the lyricism that lay on her soul.

I am the inheritor of twenty black, zippered notebooks filled with my mother's language, sonnets and free verse and a new form she created, the burtonelle. There is a nearly finished manuscript titled *Living with Joy*, an unpublished book of love poems, letters and filing cabinets and several years of daily journals—all my mother's writings.

Obviously this has influenced me, but I am also aware that had my parents been mute, even illiterate, I would have written or at least have been a teller of folk tales. I am convinced that the urge to express is impressed in the composite of my DNA.

Mother's influence in my life is more subtle, more profound than merely encouraging me to take pen to paper. It was her vision of life, her voice—to use writer's terminology, the intimate viewpoint of the author as he communicates through word form—that has incomprehensibly formed my own worldview and, consequently, molded my writing by means of which I will probably never really be aware.

In many ways, mother's background was disadvantaged. She was born in Des Moines, Iowa, December 1, 1912, to Nellie Brown Wicklund and Robert Wicklund. Her father was a lightning rod salesman who turned to drink after watching a youth in his employ fall to death while fixing rods to the pitched roof of a building.

Mother said that the memories from these years were too painful to share, and she never did speak specifically of them to me but only alluded to the fear and shame caused by her father's alcoholism. During her late teens, he converted to Christianity and was miraculously enabled to overcome his alcoholism, but within a year, he had died of pneumonia, leaving behind a family of five with no visible means of support.

At this time, mother gave up plans for college and went to work to help support her family. Eventually, her own body rebelled at the stress of death and poverty and anxiety. She became a victim of the rheumatic fever that damaged her heart. She recovered and returned to work. After some years, the literary fiancee entered, then exited, then my father appeared.

At this point, as well as I can construct, there evolved a determination on my parents' part that they were not going to live their life together hampered by an invalid mentality.

That is the profound influence that has shaped me more than mother's dogged question, "Karen, what are you writing?" It was this remarkable conspiracy on the part of my parents to daily choose life over death, despite the disadvantages of their backgrounds, the many emotional quirks of their own personalities, or the potential negations in their circumstances.

Mother was a romantic, a poetical lyricist who saw moondust and apple blossoms in all of life, who endowed her closest associates, her friends and children with superhuman qualities, then was disillusioned when the moondust was discovered to be artificial kleig lights, when the poison spray on the apple trees killed the birds, and when the gods and goddesses of her world displayed plain human tendencies.

She felt everything deeply, was intuitive, sensitive, and idealistic. She accumulated learning by osmosis and without a master plan, and she was dependent upon my father's cool logic and psychological analysis to interpret to her the factual, realistic meaning of the world, and of the people in it.

Dad was rudder to mother's sailing ship. He was also most frequently her ballast. Interestingly, she came into her own after the ballast had been pirated and her rudder snapped by high seas. Three months after their joint retirement, my father became ill with encephalitis, infection to the brain itself.

The years mother spent as an executive secretary while I was a child, later an adolescent, and then newly married are not as integral to an understanding of her personal influence on me as were her later years.

I often regret my parents' inability to recognize mother's very real creative abilities earlier, that she used her gifts typing letters and board reports, composing newsletters. Heavily involved in parachurch organizations, each of my parents held to a ministry mentality. They both actively served their Lord full-time, in ways that eventually bore fruit in the lives of their own children. All three of us are ministering families. My brother is a pastor. My sister is married to a minister as am I.

When I feel disappointment about this lack of vision regarding mother's gifts, I soon remind myself that neither of my parents had the parents I had.

It was in those agonizing years following the shipwreck which cast my father's body and personality, broken and disordered, upon the shores that the meaning of my mother's life became focused to me. Under this extreme stress, illness and dementia and death, mother's flaws and strengths became exaggerated, clear for me to examine and see.

For a time, mother needed all her energies. She was flailing in high waters. During this rationing of personality, I often felt the loss of both parents. But even in those early days of illness, those slow hours of inquisition in the hospital when doctors searched for a diagnosis and my father's condition rapidly worsened until he was nothing but a comatose form whose chest the nurses punched to regulate the irregular pull of lungs—even then, mother wrote poetry in the waiting rooms. These poems, about long hospital corridors and wildernesses of the soul, became the basis for her book, *I Need a Miracle Today, Lord.*

SONNET OF THE MIDGET CROSSES

To die upon a charred and burning cross—
I am unworthy, Lord, the martyr's name!
To count all this world's gain but pauper loss,
    could my weak soul bear out the Hus-like shame:
Each day holds midget crosses, one by one.
Let me not flinch, as fingers point the match,
    and I, the object of my torment's fun,
    behold the blue-white flame leap from the scratch.
As the wood chars deep within my soul,
    burn out the worthless chaff of my desire:
the choking dross of every human goal
be now consumed upon Your altar fire.
    And through the midget crosses of each day,
    let me now walk the living martyr's way.

I am convinced that the miracle of my mother, Wilma Burton, was that after shipwreck, after floundering on the sands of a castaway's shore, she eventually built her own little boat, unfurled her mast, and plied her way, alone, back onto the open sea.

Obviously, the going was not smooth sailing. Storms swamped her little dinghy. Further hurricanes cast her overboard; she lost her balance and frequently swallowed bitter salt water, but, amazingly, mother always climbed back into the bobbing vessel, dried herself out, set sail, and caught a windstream.

In the face of adversity, mother's tenacity was remarkable. What would have drowned a lesser person became ocean for mother to swim. The life pattern of refusing to be invalid in any way, in body or in emotion or in spirit, became her survival vest. Having lost her human rudder, my father, I watched her increasing dependency on the Ocean Master, the One who controls all the waves.

Not only did she hold on, her tenacity became productive.

LET THERE BE NO GRAY
CURTAINS TODAY, LORD

shutting out Your face
and the world of light
on light on light that You
have made.
    This world has far too many curtains:
    iron, bamboo and ghetto
    to name a few, but purple curtains
    of the heart and gray ones of the mind
    are far more prevalent.
Defying boundaries
they suddenly appear
and hang on rods of words
or lack of words
to do their silent work
of shutting in and shutting out.
    Yours the hands adept
    at rending curtains
    in temples of stone or flesh:
Let there be no curtains, Lord, today.

Making decisions on her own was one of the areas in which she floundered. She had never made a major purchase without consultation with my father. Just mention "mother buying a car" in my family and brows lift, eyes roll in an appeal toward heaven. Oh, the convolutions of complications she invented! Car-buying became the symbol on which hung all the haplessness of her awkward non-widowhood. The act became akin to an emotional cyclone. She over-researched the products, reading endless consumer reports, discussing increasing options with friends, conferring with her children *ad infinitum*—and taking *none* of our advice. One wanted to shout, "Buy it! Buy anything! Take our car!"

A purchase was finally made, but not until the whole family had been involved in weeks of emotional indecision, which we discovered to be typical for a while of most of her decision-making.

How often mother would phone, those early morning calls, swamped by some improbable storm of personal dilemma. "I need something good to happen today," she would wail. Stress had made her forget that we humans are empowered to create our own good happenings.

After time, mother learned to negotiate the decision-making seas. The next car, a few years later, was purchased with a minimum of advice seeking, and she even bought something slightly impractical, something my father would not have chosen.

Three or four years after my father's initial illness, she was a far different woman than the one she had been. Entering vigorously into the world of publishing, she established a wide circle of friends, fellow poets, and writers. She traveled the country conducting poetry workshops and speaking in writers' conferences. Her responsibilities as the editor of *The Pen Woman* took her to Washington, D.C., for national board meetings. She learned to manage the properties my father had left awaiting his attention until retirement, the family residence, the ninety-four-acre farm, a small rental property, the trailer in Florida.

During all this, she continued to make daily trips to the nursing home except for winters, which she spent in the south because the severe northern climate aggravated her anginal heart condition. While my father was still ambulatory, mother attempted to get him outside of the institutional environment as much as possible. She brought him home, took him out to restaurants, to concerts, to supermarkets—anything to prevent vegetation. Navigating a brain-damaged, incontinent adult was an undertaking demanding incredible power of will and deep loyalty.

My father's condition slowly degenerated, however, despite all efforts, and mother's professional life blossomed against the private torture which increased proportionately to the degree of my father's dementia.

Actually, an intriguing phenomenon was occurring in my mother. The sociological process of self-actualization which normally takes place in the twenties and thirties was going on in mother in her late fifties and sixties. All becomings are awkward; when they are three decades late, they may at times look preposterous.

Jokingly, my oldest child would call her "my teenage grandmother." The two of them considered this verbal badge to be one of commendation, and though I laughed, I was sometimes chagrined by how near the truth it was.

At times, mother's emerging propensities looked decidedly auntie-mamish. She loved gatherings of people, was garrulous and animated, never considered at any time that she might be an outsider, thought nothing of pushing her own books and accomplishments, was an unabashed name-dropper, often monopolized conversations.

Once Craig had mother come for Sunday dinner along with another woman her age from his church. When asked for a report on how the afternoon had proceeded he replied, "Oh, just fine! Mother talked. The other woman talked. Neither of them listened for a moment to what the other was saying and they *both* had a wonderful time!"

Mother spent hours on the phone with her friends, and my sister and I detected a generational style of dress that began to develop. Valerie dubbed it "dowdy-queen-of-England." Jewelry was worn for jewelry's sake, never to particularly accessorize an outfit, and large hats began to emerge as a costume must.

We noticed that she slightly stretched the truth to enlarge the reputation of her children. All events were marked with poetry, *her poetry,* sometimes decoupaged, sometimes unpolished.

Without my father to interpret humans for her, to enlarge their fatal flaws with laughter, mother was often snowed by some obnoxious types—like the woman who said she was Elvis Presley's aunt. She may have been, for all I know. I took her with a grain of salt; mother swallowed her hook, line, and sinker. She was particularly susceptible to the self-proclaimed "artist" types. She believed everyone's press releases, like the gentleman who specialized in sculpturing madonnas. His home was filled with his own art. Mother thought he was marvelous.

Mother was so caught up, on the one hand, with the crisis that was my father, and on the other hand, with her thrilling emerging professionalism, that until her death, I never again felt that I had her full attention. If I had read something, it reminded her of something *she* had read. If I had a personal achievement, she was more enthusiastic about her own. Finally I stopped telling, opting to wait until this too had passed.

Once, during those years, I had her full attention. One of the children, doing an experiment in the backyard, ignited the gasoline in the lawn-mower can. Attempting to beat out the flames which were charring the backside of our house, the child was burned himself.

Because we had been having a series of near brushes with death, I fell apart over this minor disaster, crying over the phone, painting the horror of my blackened world.

Mother was sympathetic, made warm noises, rushed over with dinner. Somehow this fleeting restoration of roles stabilized my sanity. For a while, I was child; mother was parent.

The more that mother self-authenticated, the more I individuated. We were both come-lately in certain sociological processes. The problem with having loving, supportive parents is that a child feels no need to cut umbilical ties. One must separate in order to find identity, the way my mother discovered who she was after my father's illness.

My identity demanded separateness at this time of my mother's own self-discovery. In some ways, it was painful to us both, and without her interpreter, my father, to explain the psychological journey we were both undertaking, I think mother was wounded by me without knowing exactly why. (Without Dad, mother had no one to tell her that the gentleman with all the madonnas was, (1) not a very good artist, and (2) looney as a bird to boot!)

Enough of this insistence on truth. All saints are strange. All holy things are wacky.

So what that mother took up bicycle riding and broke her ankle—I gave her the bicycle! No matter that my sister gave her a lovely pleated houserobe and she wore it (belted) to a formal dinner. ("She didn't!" protested my sister. "She did," I replied. "I have a picture right here. She received a prize or something.")

No matter that she not only dropped her names, she dropped *our* names, the well-known people *we* had met or associated with, names we children would never mention ourselves, all of us being extremely diffident.

So what if she and her friends went traipsing off to all corners and mother thought they were all raving beauties and people of accomplishment. So what if her romantic frame of mind prevented her from understanding that she was getting old. No, she was ageless; her associates were ageless.

So what if we children were sometimes embarrassed and had to "come to terms."

So what if all of our friends loved our auntie-mame mother. My sister once offered a helpful explanation: "It's not at all threatening if it's not your mother acting that way."

We continually heard from them: "Your mother's such a character." "Your mother is simply fascinating." "Your mother is so warm and loving."

I am well aware, student of human nature that I am, that all of our weaknesses are only the shadow side of our strengths.

This garrulous woman was also a woman of great verbal intelligence who could converse on a wide range of topics with a wide variety of people. Her learning never peaked; it never reached a high-water mark, then began to recede. Without higher education herself, she taught poetry symposiums on many a college campus.

She loved people and even though she tended to romanticize them, her positive approval brought out many of their best points. She collected friends by the tens and hundreds. I was continually amazed by the quantities (if not always the qualities) of my mother's friends.

She was quick-witted. At one writers' conference, she saved a man's life by administering CPR after he suffered a heart attack. I was in her kitchen the day roses from his wife were delivered. The card read something like, "For the gift of the life of my husband." Mother burst into tears.

She loved life and participated in it fully, never conserving herself, never really recognizing her own limitations (she suffered her limitations, but she never recognized them). "Let's go ... let's do something interesting," were some of her favorite phrases. She never came to terms with the truth that you fall as low emotionally as you rise high. She was often depleted from her expenditures of energy. It confused her. "I don't know why I'm feeling so exhausted," she would comment. The reasons were obvious to everyone but herself.

Mother was always up hours before the rest of the world. She wrote in her diary, composed poetry, prayed. Often by the time the rest of us were functioning, she had worked on the magazine, written a chapter for a book, picked strawberries or made rice pudding, noticed birdsong, watched the sun rise. It was wonderful, really, her loving the gift of life so.

My firstborn, the one five decades younger than his grandmother, named her Dobie when he was barely lisping his first words; and Dobie she became to all the grandchildren. My children loved her. They were like my friends—if it's not your own mother doing those outrageous things, it's not embarrassing.

The teens gave a party and mother chaperoned because I was out of town. "Really, Mother!" reported my daughter. "I think we should have had a chaperone for Dobie. She had as much fun as the kids. And she got kind of carried away during the scrabble marathon. You should have seen the words she was using."

They all have Dobie stories. Every outing with her ended in misadventure.

Mother *always* emerged from under her flood waters because she loved life. She greeted this great gift of life each new day. She taught me to identify the lovely, anguished gift of being. With a leaking heart and a brain-damaged husband, the real Wilma Burton nevertheless emerged, with all her vagaries and wonder. She chased after life, she chased it hard.

Mother was a woman of deep faith who verbalized it with the greatest of ease on all occasions, with strangers and with familiars. She saw the holiness in the firm world around her, struggled to find it in its bramble side as well.

I AM NOT SATISFIED WITH CRUMBS

from Your banquet table.
I would know Your full-course meal
complete with aperitif
of sweet communion wine
and over all the frescoed banner
of Your love
　stretching
from dawn to sunset
with the sunlit, starlit, moonlit
wonder of Your presence.

Mother was square-dancing the night she died. She was planning to remarry. Some of her last words were, "Isn't this fun?"

She slid suddenly from her chair and was gone—but I know that on my birthday, a death she had anticipated thirty-nine years before, she went dancing into heaven.

With a heritage such as this, who am I to fear forty?

Mother was a woman of deep faith, a faith that was tested in the last years of her life. Many people of deep faith become serene and sedate as they age. Mother just became more of herself, and with that she honored her Creator.

Actually, serene and sedate saints are rather dull.

Despite the aberrations, I would rather age like my mother. None of this sweet little old lady bit for me. I would rather be a tough old bird—but holy.

Mother never stopped becoming. Please God, neither shall I.

Mrs. O. with Madeleine L'Engle's first child, Josephine.

NINE

Mary McKenna O'Connell

by Madeleine L'Engle

IT IS MY GREAT PRIVILEGE to have known a saint. She was not, perhaps, an obvious candidate for sainthood (like Dorothy Day, or one of her own favorites, Mother Seton), because she lived a life of almost complete anonymity. But nobody who had the privilege of knowing her will ever forget her. And she is probably the most powerful single spiritual influence in my life.

After her death I was given her simple rosary, and it is one of my greatest treasures, the beads worn with prayer. But when Mary McKenna O'Connell looked at the cross it was not to weep over the wounds but to laugh with the joy of the resurrection. The joy of the living Christ shone from her, putting all the events of life into perspective and proportion.

She came into my life, and as a great blessing, very early. My parents had been childless for nearly twenty years before my mother was able to complete a pregnancy and bring forth a live and healthy baby.

Mother told me that once she and Father had had their long-awaited baby, I became a bone of contention between them. They disagreed completely on how I ought to be brought up.

Father wanted a strict English childhood for me, and this is more or less what I got—nanny, governesses, supper on a tray in the nursery, dancing lessons, music lessons, skating lessons, art lessons . . .

Mother had the idea that she wanted me trained by a circus performer, that it would give me grace and coordination and self-assurance, but Father was horrified. I wish Mother had had her way. However, I did have Mrs. O.

Mrs. O., Nanny: odd, obsolete, un-American idea. But Mrs. O. is worth a book in herself. She was English, a Liverpudlian. I was always comfortably certain that she loved me, but it was a typically Anglo-Saxon love which did not indulge in demonstrativeness. She did not, as I remember, kiss me at bedtime when I was a small child. One of our pleasant jokes, after my marriage, was Hugh's attempts to give her a kiss; despite much laughter, she managed to avoid the kisses. Nor was she ever a handholder.

Her family for generations had belonged to the highest order of English servants—and there is nothing more rigid or more snobbish than the English servant class system. It started to break down during World War I and vanished during World War II. There are a few nannies left, but not many. Mine was ninety-one the summer my mother died, still completely *compos mentis*, and passionately concerned with all the doings of my family. She clucked with me many times about Mother's decline, and somehow she always managed to phone me on a day when things had been particularly difficult, and by the end of the conversation we were both laughing.

She was born Mary McKenna and came to the New World when she was fifteen, to spend a summer on Prince Edward Island taking care of four small children. At summer's end she went to visit one of her aunts, who was housekeeper for a wealthy family on Park Avenue; the enormous house is still in existence, now a club. There were four in the family, and forty on the staff, which included gardeners, coachmen, and outdoor laborers. The staff ate dinner at noon, around a long table below stairs, having a "joint" each day, bowls of potatoes, vegetables, salad. They were well-fed, if hard-worked. The family dined at night. One of the daughters of

the family, Miss Amy, fourteen, was blind as a result of scarlet
fever. She was spoiled and demanding. Young Mary McKenna's
aunt suggested that Mary take Miss Amy for a walk. When Miss
Amy began to be difficult, not wanting to walk, whining and
demanding to go home, Mary said, "My aunt said that you are
supposed to walk for an hour, doctor's orders."

Miss Amy said, "I won't."

Mary said, "You will."

Miss Amy said, "I'll lie down in the street."

Mary said, "Go ahead, for all the good it will do you." It was the
first time anybody had crossed Miss Amy since her blindness.

They walked for a full hour, and when they got home Miss Amy
said to her mother, "I want Mary."

So Mary McKenna, barely older than blind Miss Amy, became a
lady's maid. The next day the family left for a trip abroad, and Mary
sat at the captain's table with Miss Amy, to help her. The family
arrived in Paris earlier than expected, and the floor of the hotel
which was usually reserved for their use had not yet been emptied,
so the servants were sent, just for one night, up to the top of the
hotel, under the eaves.

Mary McKenna announced to one of the others, "I've never slept
in a place like this before, and I'm not going to begin now." So she
went looking for some way to summon help and express her
displeasure. At one end of the attic she saw a series of brass bells,
took a broomstick and began whacking away at them, making a
considerable din. It was not until firemen came rushing upstairs
with hoses and hatchets that she knew which bells she had rung.

However, she had made her point. She did not sleep in the attic.

With Miss Amy she traveled all over Europe, went to formal
dinner parties, to the opera, to the theatre; because of Miss Amy's
blindness she saw far more of the above-stairs world than would
most lady's maids.

Then she met and married John O'Connell, whose brother is still
remembered in Ireland as one of the great fighters of the Irish
revolution. They had three daughters, and then the O'Connell
family fell on hard times, and in order to help feed and clothe the
children she went back to work, and the only work she could get

was as a charwoman—the lowest rung of the English servant caste system. It was a humiliation to her that few could understand.

She worked on Wall Street cleaning offices at night. My godfather often worked late and got to talking with this rather unusual cleaning woman, and once when his wife was having a large party and needed extra help, he asked Mrs. O'Connell if she could come to their house and help out. My parents were at that party, and later Mother phoned to find out who the splendid extra helper had been, and if she would come help at a party Mother and Father were giving.

When she arrived at our apartment, Mother smiled and said, "I don't even know your name."

"My name is Mrs. O'Connell, but I expect you will want to call me Mary."

"I'd be delighted to call you Mrs. O'Connell," Mother said, and that was the beginning of a friendship between the two women, and my nanny's entrance into my life. I was only a baby, and when I began to talk I called her "O," and a little later "Mrs. O," and Mrs. O she has remained, and there are many people who don't know her by any other name. Wherever she was, she brought laughter, and a sense of fun, although her life, after she left Miss Amy, was full of pain and tragedy.

Until arthritis prevented her from traveling, she spent several weeks with us, three or four times a year, and I treasure a small snapshot of Mother and Mrs. O sitting on the sofa, side by side, nattering away. They shared many of the same memories—of operas all over Europe, of singers; Mrs. O refers casually to Madam Melba, Jean de Reszke, Chalijapin. If Mother knew the people above-stairs, so did Mrs. O, and from the point of view of below-stairs, so she was able to tell Mother all kinds of little tidbits she'd never have heard otherwise. She also enjoyed telling stories on herself, such as the time she was sent out to buy pâté de foie gras; when she reached the grocer she couldn't remember the French words, "but it sounds like Paddy Fogarty." The closest she has ever come to being vulgar is when she said, "Ah, well, I must go and shed a tear for Ireland," and headed for the bathroom.

She thought my father a prince, and treated him accordingly. She loved to tell of one summer when Mother and I were out of the city and Father was preparing to sail to Europe on an assignment. He couldn't find some things he needed, and knew that Mrs. O would know where they were. She didn't have a phone, so he sent her a telegram: "Come at once."

She came, and there he was, she said, sitting alone at the dining table, eating scrambled eggs by candlelight.

She also liked to tell of the times she met him on the street, when he would stand leaning on his cane and passing the time of day, "as though he didn't have anything better to do."

She was deeply religious, in a quiet way, and sometimes when she had a special concern on her mind, she would take me to church with her. She also thought—quite rightly—that I was overprotected, and took me on my first subway rides. She didn't like the fact that Mother would allow no sugar in my breakfast oatmeal; Mother always tasted the oatmeal to make sure no softhearted member of the household had sugared it; Mrs. O got around that by putting the sugar in the bottom of the porringer, and the oatmeal on top of it, and stirring it in after the porridge had been tasted, and Mother never knew, until we told her a few years ago, why I would always eat my oatmeal for Mrs. O. For I never told of the subway rides, or the visits to church, or the sugar in the cereal, or the little packets of butterscotch in the park; all I knew then and all I know now is that Mrs. O never taught me anything but good.

I used to say to her, "Will you help me take care of my children when I grow up?" And she would remind me of this on her visits to us.

When *A Night to Remember*, about the sinking of the *Titanic*, was on television, she sat and watched and rocked and clucked; she knew most of the passengers from Miss Amy's family; the captain had been to the house many a time for dinner, and the young Mary would go to the ship bearing the invitation; some of the crew she knew this way, and some from family and acquaintances in Liverpool; the movie seemed to have been filmed especially for her, and all of us watching it with her were far more moved by it than if we had not been seeing it through her eyes.

She was probably the most normal part of my childhood, and I will always be grateful for her. I think I realized that I was a subject of disagreement between my parents, and yet I managed to think that both of them were always right, and I'm sure Mrs. O had something to do with this.

The day after my mother died, I phoned one of Mrs. O's daughters, and she immediately said that she would call her mother and have her call me, which was a wise decision. When Mrs. O got on the phone she was in charge, telling me what to do, just as she had done all my life.

Last spring Mrs. O was ninety-five, and for the past several years has been in a home for elderly nuns, the Convent of Mary the Queen.

Two of her three daughters are nuns, Sister Miriam Ambrose and Sister Anastasia Marie, and it was because of them that she was given her pleasant room and bath. During these years of her old age I have been called three times to her deathbed, and each time she has surprised doctors and nurses by recovering. It isn't that she is clinging to life, like a brown and brittle leaf clinging to the tree; she is very ready to go home. When she has been on the road to recovery she has each time remarked with good-humored resignation, "Well, God doesn't want me and the devil won't have me."

The Sisters call me regularly to report on her condition, and we all try to go see her as often as possible, and to bring the little girls, my granddaughters, for a state visit once a year. This spring she became very weak, and her mind began to wander, but the Sisters urged me not to come. "If there's a day when she's alert and will recognize you, we'll call."

In August I suddenly had a tremendous urge to go to her, and my friend Gillian said that she'd love to take a day off from work and drive to the convent with me. So when Sister Ambrose called to say that her mother seemed a little stronger and might recognize me, we decided to go.

It was a brilliant summer day. There had been a lot of rain, so the leaves were a lush rich green, not dry and dusty as they sometimes are in August.

When we reached the convent, I fell silent. A voice called

upstairs on a loudspeaker to announce our visit. We walked through a long room with two rows of rocking chairs where ancient Sisters sit to watch television. When Hugh comes to the convent with me, it is an added glory for Mrs. O, for not only do the Sisters watch his show, but most of the nurses, and many of them come hurrying for autographs or simply to shake hands with "Dr. Tyler."

Gillian and I go up on the elevator to the fourth floor. Mrs. O's room is just around the corner. From there she has been able to watch all the comings and goings on the floor. It is hot in the summer, and we have wanted to give her an air-conditioner, but she won't have one because she'd have to keep her door closed and thus be isolated from the life bustling around her.

Wherever she is, she always brings with her the gift of laughter. The nurses on the night shift say, when they are tired or discouraged, "I think I'll go to Mrs. O'Connell's room. She's always good for a laugh." The orderlies and cleaning women love her; whenever there has been a crisis in her condition there have been tears, open and unashamed. Perhaps she is being kept here on earth for so long because her gift of laughter is desperately needed. Ill and difficult patients may well be treated with more tenderness because of Mrs. O.

Never very large, each year she has become smaller and smaller. But there is today a startling change since my last visit. She has eaten nothing solid for three months; a little tea, a little thin soup, the Holy Mysteries; on these she has been kept alive. But there is nothing now between skin and bones. The body on the hospital bed looks like pictures of victims of Belsen, Auschwitz, Ravensbruck.

When I first bend over her she does not know me. I wait while she makes the slow journey from the past to the present. I put my hand on hers and say, "It's Madeleine, Mrs. O. It's Madeleine." Suddenly she is fully with me, and she puts her arms around me as she would never have done in the old days, and says, "Oh, Madeleine, my Madeleine, oh, my Madeleine," and I no longer see the ancient wasted body. I have my arms about her so that I am holding her sitting up, with the fragile body leaning against me like a child's, and yet she is still holding me; we are both child, both mother.

She moves in and out of time. We talk in low voices and she asks me how the children are. Does Bion still have his nice girlfriend? How are the little girls? She hasn't seen Gillian for at least fifteen years and yet she is completely aware of her presence and knows who she is, and asks about her family.

Once she gets lost in chronology and asks me, "Are you downstairs in your carriage?" But the next moment she is back in the present and says, "How's the boss?" (Her pet name for Hugh.) "How could I have forgotten to ask about the boss?"

I stay for an hour, much longer than I had expected, but we are in *kairos,* Mrs. O and I, in God's time, free, for the rest of the hour, from *chronos.* "And the extraordinary thing," I wrote in my journal, "was the electric current of love, powerful and beautiful, flowing back and forth between Mrs. O and me. Gillie had expected to step outside and write letters, but she too felt the lovely light of love which was uniting Mrs. O and me, so she stayed, remarking later what a privilege it had been for her to be present. I cannot set down in words the strength and joy of that river of love; it was something which can happen only in *kairos;* it was a time of Transfiguration—and in the octave of Transfiguration, too—I just thought about that."

So we are given our glimpses of what it is really like, how things are really meant to be. There in that wasted body I saw at the same time the transfigured body, something visible to the spirit and not to the eyes.

These glimpses of reality are the foundation stones of faith.

Mrs. O was, for me, *is* for me, a true saint. As far as worldly success is concerned, she is nobody. But she knows who she is. She had no hesitation in ringing the fire bells of an elegant Paris hotel if she didn't think her quarters fitting. She was not overawed by hobnobbing with the Greats in the world of opera or theatre or society. She simply took it for granted. If she liked people, she liked them on her own terms, regardless of their public reputation. It never occurred to her that her opinion was not valid. She had a totally unselfconscious and humble sense of *amour propre.*

But perhaps the most telling quality of sainthood is laughter. She brought laughter with her, no matter how serious or tragic the surroundings. Since in God's good time "all shall be well and all shall be well and all manner of things shall be well" (as Lady Julian of Norwich, another of my favourite saints, and a remarkably liberated woman, wrote in the fifteenth century), there is nothing that cannot in some measure be redeemed by holy laughter.

She would have been comfortably at home with St. Teresa of Avila. And she would have been equally at home with the other Thérèse, the Little Flower. Because her true home was heaven (and heaven was wherever God chose to put her, no matter how hellish to the casual observer it might seem), there was no place on earth where she was not comfortably at home. And there was no place where she did not bring her gift of loving, compassionate laughter. And, with Mrs. O, laughter was always with and for, never *at.* It was always healing, never destructive.

I have known many women more important in the world's eyes than Mary McKenna O'Connell. Like Jesus, she was not interested in causes, or starting movements which would bring her prominence, but she was passionately interested in people. Anyone who came into her orbit received the gift of a greater sense of self than they had had before; they felt more named, more real. And that is the gift of the saint, for that reality is always tied in with an awareness that we are God's, children of light, meant to walk in the light. I will always be grateful that in my own lifetime I have known a true saint, and have been made more real by that knowing.

And I am certain that she is giving the angels some good laughs, and that there is more joy in heaven because of her presence.

TEN

Ethel Renwick

by Rebecca Manley Pippert

IF ONLY MY PARENTS could find happiness, I thought, then I would be happy too. I was a teenager, watching their marriage dissolve. What I had believed to be the most secure aspect of our life together was in fact the least. But the pain I experienced drove me to ultimate questions. When everything seemed at peace again (although they later divorced), I was still left feeling a strange, gnawing emptiness. I was surprised to realize that what I had longed for the most, a secure family structure, was simply not big enough to build my life upon. So the search began for a foundation strong and trustworthy enough on which to base my life. Although the roots of my search were emotional, the process itself was intellectual.

I studied every system of thought I came across—philosophies, world religions—everything, that is, *except* Christianity. I assumed I knew about Christianity. After all, hadn't I been raised in America? I had even been a Girl Scout!

Although I was raised with a great deal of love, ours was not a particularly religious home. I went to Sunday school and to church sporadically as a young teen. But Evangelical theology and lifestyle were foreign to me.

Everything I studied left me unsatisfied, even despairing. I had wanted logical, defensible answers. I recall asking a believer how he knew his faith was true. "It's a feeling in my heart," he said.

"But what about my head? I have a head as well as a heart!" I exclaimed.

Then I stumbled across a book I was surprised to find in my family's library, *Mere Christianity* by C.S. Lewis. In Lewis I found myself face-to-face with an intellect so disciplined, so lucid, so relentlessly logical, that all of my intellectual pride at not being a "mindless simple believer" was quickly squelched.

I read Lewis, line by line, with intensity and hunger. The issue finally became clear: Could Jesus really be God? Not a prophet, a great teacher, but *God himself?* My conclusion was twofold: First, if Jesus was God, then the final proof of his God-nature must be his physical resurrection. Second, a Christian was one who not only believed in this Jesus, but actually *knew* him. And if those two propositions were true, then as far as I could tell, I had never met a Christian. At least I had never met anyone who talked about knowing Jesus personally. I poured out my frustrations to my pastor, Malcolm Nygren, whom I had not seen in a long time. His final words were, "Come to Sunday school. There's a couple you must meet."

I walked into class that morning feeling awkward. I wanted solid answers, not pat Sunday school rhetoric. Without knowing it, I took a seat next to the teacher—a tall, dignified woman named Ethel Renwick. She was elegant, bright-eyed, and chock full of energy. Her graciousness put me at ease immediately.

Three questions burned in me. But before I had a chance to ask them, she answered them—in sequence. And she answered them well. I was spellbound. As I ventured to ask her other questions, she seemed to take genuine delight in them. I was intrigued to realize that this woman, with so vast a knowledge of the world, was yet a convinced Christian.

She began to talk about knowing Jesus—not as an ethic, or a code of laws, but as a *living* Lord. As I watched her, I perceived a radiance and a presence that spoke to my depths. I felt drawn to her in a way I had never experienced with anyone else. Suddenly it dawned on me that this inexplicable attraction I felt was not to her—it was to Christ in her. Christ *must* have risen, I thought, because he is so alive in her! It was my first glimpse of Jesus, and I loved him instantly. My mind and my heart connected. It was true and I knew it. Relief and joy flooded me as I said to God, "This is it. This really is it. I'm home . . . at last."

I had just been converted.

That afternoon I drove over to her house and drank in her words as she read scripture to me. We met together uncounted times in the weeks that followed, reading the Bible and praying. I grew to know her family well. Her husband, Frank, and their three children, George, Margo, and Robert, have all played significant roles in my life. From that Sunday morning fifteen years ago until now, a day has not passed when Ethel has not prayed for me. What impressed me then still impresses me. She is a woman who has fallen hopelessly in love with God. She celebrates his world and the gifts he has given us to enjoy. And she respects the way he intends life to be lived. I have never once heard her give a glib answer. She is a model of godly wholeness.

One of five children, Ethel was raised in Chicago. Her father, Milan Hulbert, was a noted architect and inventor, decorated by eight countries. Her mother, Olive, was an American raised in Europe, an artist fluent in five languages. She was the President of Alliance Francaise and one of only two women outside of France ever to receive the French Legion of Honor. The other woman, Madame Curie, was a personal friend.

Prior to World War II, Madame Curie came to America to promote the French Red Cross. During her stay, she stood in endless reception lines, always shaking hands with her gloves on. Underneath those gloves were hands badly eaten by radium. But when it came time to say goodbye to Ethel's mother, she took off her gloves to embrace her—a poignant gesture from an otherwise restrained and quiet woman.

Ethel can remember the infectious excitement among the servants and the children whenever special guests came. They would peek over the banister for a glimpse of Sarah Bernhart or Madame Curie.

By training, Ethel was herself more European than American.

She spoke only French until she entered school. Each child in the Hulbert family had a governess to take care of practical needs so that the parents could devote extra time to developing their children's minds and forming their values. Ethel remembers her home as a place of great security and love, where discipline was firm, but love stronger.

Dinner time was a cherished event. Everyone dressed for dinner, wearing a coat and tie or a dress. During the meal, her father would introduce a topic and a lively discussion would ensue. Each child was expected to be well-read and conversant, and all opinions were regarded with respect.

The atmosphere in the Hulbert home was one of tremendous curiosity, characterized by a fervor for knowledge and truth and a deep appreciation of other cultures and ways of life. Each member of the family played an instrument, and together they formed a family orchestra, with Olive Hulbert on the harp and Milan Hulbert on the cello.

Life was good and meant to be appreciated. "Never be afraid of truth," her father would say. He made it a practice never to punish the children for telling the truth.

The children's manners were impeccable, and their mother taught them that good manners were a reminder that others were important. She instructed them to make life as easy as possible for others. "Manners are always motivated by thoughtfulness to others—a reminder that we are not the center of the universe," she would say.

Ethel's parents were Episcopalians who trained their children in the ways of the church. But it was not their custom to discuss faith and God. They baptized their children, sent them to Sunday school, and taught them to say their prayers. Faith was assumed, not probed.

Two events in Ethel's life proved to have a profound impact on her. The first happened when she was only thirteen years old. A team of physicians in Chicago had examined her father and concluded that he had only six months to live. Ethel remembers the verdict: "There is nothing medicine can do." The children were packed off to boarding schools while the parents, following doctors' orders, went to California. Rather than give up all hope of recovery, Milan Hulbert studied nutrition and devised a diet based on whole grains and other natural foods. "The doctors said it wouldn't help," Ethel recalled. "But it did and he lived to a ripe old age."

While Ethel was at boarding school, her father sent her wheat germ and bran. "Sprinkle this stuff on your cereal," he wrote. His advice hardly seems remarkable today, but it was astonishing for the 1930s. The impact of her father's cure and his determination to eat natural foods was to have far-reaching implications for Ethel's life and ministry.

Another major event in her life took place in 1932. Her father's view of education, much akin to his pioneer spirit, was that life was meant to be understood and experienced. He wanted his children to see the whole of life—not to perceive it simply through American eyes. To achieve this goal, he encouraged them to travel, to visit different countries, meet the people, study the language, religion, and food. "While my parents' friends spent enormous amounts of money on elaborate balls for their daughters," explained Ethel, "my parents supported us in our endeavors to appreciate and understand the world."

Mrs. Hulbert and her four tall daughters journeyed not once but three times around the world. In those days, travel was fairly primitive and slow, which meant that the four women had ample time to study the various countries and cultures in which they found themselves. Ethel had always been especially interested in philosophy and religion in college. Now she was able to study each religion close up. She was fascinated by what she saw, and she realized, subsequently, that she was searching for God even then.

The five travelers embarked on their journeys prior to the spread of communism and the spread of industrialization to many of the remote regions of the world. They took freighters through tropical isles and rode narrow-gauge railroads and all manner of motor vehicles across distant landscapes. They sat atop elephants as they swayed through the jungles of the deserted city of Rajputan, blazing with vivid colors and reverberating with the cries of the wild peacocks, parrots, and monkeys. Later, the five women booked passage on an onion freighter, which sailed through the South Pacific, stopping at Borneo and the exotic islands of Mindanao, Jolo, Zamboagna, and Ilo Ilo.

Her father's approach to eating made Ethel curious about the food people ate. The most elaborate meal she encountered was hosted by the burgomaster of Brussels and consisted of eight courses, including everything from pâtè to bombe.

But they ate the simplest and probably the most nutritious meal seated on the ground with a tribal chief of Iloilo, in the Philippines. There were delicious chunks of roast pork, tapioca kneaded in a large wooden trough, bread, fruit, coconut meat from the shell, and fresh vegetables steamed over hot rocks. The natives ate only what their forebears ate, and seemed strong, healthy, and happy. And they had sparkling teeth.

But on her return trips, Ethel also saw people who had converted to the Western diet. To her surprise, many of them were not only unhealthy, flabby, and surly, but their teeth were rotten as well. These people had no dentists to counteract the damage done by eating sweets and other such foods. Ethel concluded that the culprit was an unnatural diet. She has not changed her mind.

Eventually, Ethel returned to live in America. The first crisis she faced came when she was still a young adult. Like so many others in the Great Depression, her father's business failed, due in part to a dishonest employee. The Hulbert family went from having everything to nothing. Ethel was forced to go to work immediately, managing a hotel in Chicago. Her reaction to the crisis was twofold: "On the one hand our parents never let us think that money or material things were important. We were taught to value ideas, culture, music, and art. So it was not so much a devastation as a challenge. However, up until that time, my life had been fairly sheltered. I trusted people and believed they were good. But this experience forced me to see that people were not inherently good. I learned that I needed to become more astute in my judgment of character. I couldn't trust everyone I met."

Later, she met a handsome young man by the name of Frank Renwick, her brother's roommate at military academy. They married after a friendship blossomed into courtship while he studied law. Later, they settled in Colorado Springs, where Frank joined a legal firm.

Ethel was satisfied and content. Her marriage was a happy one, her three children a delight to her. She didn't question God's existence, but neither did she seek him. She sent the children to Sunday school, even though she and Frank never attended church.

One day her eldest child, George, came home from Sunday school and asked, "Mother, was Jesus really raised from the dead?" George's simple question took her by surprise. She considered herself a Christian, one whose family had placed great importance on truth. But she felt unable to answer this earnest question from her nine-year-old child.

She asked herself, "Did Jesus rise from the dead or not?" If so, she would admit the truth and proclaim it to others. If not, she would take her children out of Sunday school. She was determined to find the answer. (Fascinating to me, this same question was the one that, years later, was to drive me to her Sunday school class.)

The next Sunday, she attended church and heard a minister ask: "Did you come here to find Christ? Unless Christ lives in you, you won't find him in a building." She kept mulling over what he said. "Christ in you." But how can Christ be in a person, she pondered?

She discussed her questions with her husband. She and Frank had always been close. If one was interested in a topic then the other wanted to study it as well. They agreed that it was important to find answers. So they searched. They attended church regularly and Ethel began reading books on Christianity. What she read thrilled her.

"I knew the universe was interrelated, interdependent, and integrated. Christianity made sense of the universe by explaining that God was at the center. All of nature, all of creation obeyed God, except humans who, having their own will and intellect, went their own way and chose not to fit into his plan. For the first time I saw that sin consisted not simply of an isolated act of wrongdoing but of a state of brokenness and separation from God that resulted in our going our own way. I saw that Christ came for the purpose of making us *one* with God. Christ could live in me through his Holy Spirit abiding in me. If I followed Jesus, I could be empowered by God himself to be a part of his whole purpose for the world.

"I was thrilled to discover a system that made sense. I had seen people of other religions clamoring for God's attention. They were so terrified of God that they hung food outside their huts to keep the Devil away. I'd seen fear and superstition. Now I saw that God *wanted* to live in us. He'd sent Jesus to show us the way."

Privately, she surrendered and accepted Christ. At once, she felt peace and joy at her decision. It wasn't until two weeks later that she realized she had been converted.

In the meantime, Frank had become warden of a new chapel. At a coffee hour after the chapel service, Ethel spotted three newcomers. She was intrigued to see that they were carrying Bibles. She introduced herself and discovered that they were British— Reverend David Steele and two friends. The three seemed pleasant enough, and she quickly telephoned her Latvian cook, asking her to set three more places for dinner.

During the meal, the Renwicks learned that their guests worked for the Navigators and were in town only for the summer. As Ethel peppered the three with questions, David Steele opened his Bible, showed her a passage, and said, "Does this answer it for you?" Instead of giving her his opinion, he gave her God's Word, and God's Word spoke to her. David Steele's visit confirmed to Ethel that she had indeed become a Christian. Moreover, through them, she had been introduced to the power of the scriptures.

Ethel spoke freely to her husband about her new faith. He was eager to read what she had. With his keen legal mind and open heart, he, too, was soon convinced and converted. Their three children were, at this time, all under twelve years of age. "We didn't preach at them," Ethel says. "We simply shared our delight and joy in the Lord. Jesus was real in our home. Each child came to know God and love him. When people ask how we did it, I answer honestly that it was the grace of God. Of course we prayed daily for them and tried to live a life worthy of the Gospel. But it was God's goodness that brought each one."

Ethel and Frank were a team. If Ethel spoke to a group by herself, she could always count on Frank's prayers. And Frank could always rely on her prayers. They were immensely involved in one another's lives. They left articles and pamphlets for each other to read. When they were apart they read the same scriptures or devotional material. And when they were together, they delighted in sharing the details of their day. I recall once helping Ethel prepare an unexpected dinner. We were in a hurry, and I was a bit frantic when Frank began telling her about his day. Putting down her knife, she gave him her undivided attention. Later she confided to me, "Having dinner on time is only a *thing*, Becky. But Frank is my husband. Never put things ahead of your husband."

An intriguing aspect of their relationship had to do with the fact that they both had strong wills. Neither hesitated to state a conviction forcefully. Indeed, there is not one member of the Renwick family who could be called passive. A marriage between two strong-willed people can easily lead to frequent conflict. But this was not true of Ethel and Frank Renwick. Neither of them was volatile by nature. But more than that, they seemed to share a great oneness of mind and spirit. I remember noticing the slightest frown steal across Ethel's brow one night at dinner. Frank immediately verbalized the problem that Ethel was grappling with. Clearly, he understood what was going on in Ethel's mind.

Despite this mutual understanding, they had their share of problems to work through and lessons to learn. When I asked Ethel for advice about being a good wife while helping to juggle two busy schedules, she replied, "Be careful of too much busyness for the Lord. You can end up serving the Devil instead of God." She told me that one of her first mistakes as a young believer was to become involved in so many Christian activities that Frank began to take second place. "Living by proper priorities isn't a battle that is won once and then forgotten. It involves the daily discipline of reminding oneself who the most important people to serve and love are. You must *choose* your husband each day," she explained.

David Steele and the Navigators taught the Renwicks how to study the Bible and impressed upon them the value of memorizing scripture. After meeting David, they signed up immediately for a couple's conference led by a young minister, Dr. Richard Halverson (now chaplain to the U.S. Senate). Dick Halverson had a great

impact on both of them. He suggested that they become ac-
quainted with International Christian Leadership (the "Prayer
Breakfast" movement). When Ethel attended one of the first
Presidential Prayer Breakfasts for women she found herself sitting
next to a twinkly eyed, spunky Dutch woman by the name of
Corrie ten Boom. Corrie and she became lifelong friends, and their
friendship provided Ethel with ongoing spiritual nurture.

As a new Christian, Ethel could have been tempted to isolate
herself from her "worldly" friends. Wisdom, as well as the desire to
see others come to Christ, kept her from making that mistake.
Ethel's love for God was so radiant and apparent that her country
club friends soon noticed the change in her. She did not try to
sneak the Gospel into every conversation or to force it on people.
An approach like that was alien to her gracious nature. And she
knew that theologically it was wrong. She believed that God was
seeking others as he had sought her. She knew she was cooperating
with her Creator, so she expected him to work. She had been raised
to view the universe as a whole. Now that she was a Christian, she
saw that God was to be glorified in all of life—in her love of people,
literature, music, ideas—not just in church and Bible studies. And
because she was interested in so many things, it gave God the
opportunity to be glorified in many things.

A glance around Ethel's apartment says much about the scope of
her life. In one corner is a hand-carved elephant table from India.
On a bookshelf stands an antique piece of cloisonne china, a jade
bowl from Nepal, and a Chinese silver box. In the background is an
Italian oil-painted, three-panel screen from the 1800s. On one wall
hangs an autographed picture of Victor Hugo, a gift from him to her
parents. On another wall is a lovely portrait of "Madame Le Brun,"
painted by Ethel's mother at the Louvre. Atop a Peking rug, the
coffee table bears books about Chinese art, Quebec, and several
early maps. On the sofa lies her latest manuscript on nutrition
from a biblical basis—now a foremost passion. One need only look
around to see that she is fascinated by all of life: music, literature,
the arts, other cultures, nutrition, health, and most importantly,
faith.

By her example Ethel convinced me that for the sake of Jesus Christ we must be interesting people. If our only interest is the Bible—as marvelous and important as that is—we will find ourselves limited in our ability to relate to others and even to God himself. As Ethel related God to all of life, without imposing but simply exposing what she believed, people noticed. Her love for God was contagious.

Before long, her friends began asking questions about her faith. They even asked if she would help them understand the Bible. Feeling inadequate to the task, she told them, "I can't teach you the Bible, but I'll show you how to study it and the Bible will teach you!" From the moment of her first encounter with David Steele, she knew that the Bible could speak for itself; it was "sharper than any two-edged sword."

So began her first Bible study. She has ministered through Bible studies ever since. "Many things take place in a Bible study," she says. "First, remember that people often come from liberal but nominal religious backgrounds. They are well-educated, and yet often essentially unaware of the Gospel of Jesus Christ. So in a Bible study they see who Jesus is, what he is really like, often for the first time. And Jesus is irresistible! Furthermore, the Gospel message is spelled out. Sin is explained. They begin to see the thrill of being a Christian as well as the commitment required. As the leader, I learned firsthand that God empowers us with the Holy Spirit for his tasks."

One by one, nearly every participant in that first Bible study became a Christian. What started as a Bible study for the purpose of evangelism ended up as a Bible study to nurture and disciple new believers.

Her Bible study ministry led to a speaking ministry. Through the Prayer Breakfast movement she spoke to groups across the country. Then she and Frank moved from Colorado to Arizona, where she organized and became chairperson for the Governor's Wife's prayer luncheon, which included 800 women. Simultaneously, she started several new Bible studies, at one time leading as many as five a week.

How did she do it? She simply prayed that God would guide her to the people he was seeking. She had no strategy, other than what God provided.

Both Frank and Ethel led several classes for couples. And both had a vital ministry in Arizona, leading groups alone as well as together.

Because of her keen interest in food, Ethel wrote a book at that time entitled *A World of Good Cooking* (Simon and Schuster), which was awarded the bronze medal at the International Cookbook Fair in Frankfurt, Germany.

Then Frank was asked to be the director of the Executive Development Center at the University of Illinois. So they moved to Champaign, Illinois for two years. The reverberation of their ministry there is still being felt. In Champaign they attended a large, mainline Presbyterian church. Reverend Malcolm Nygren, the pastor who baptized me and performed my wedding and who has a unique gift for incorporating and using the gifts of others, welcomed the Renwicks warmly.

Both of them taught adult Sunday school classes, in which many, including myself, were converted. They led Bible studies and taught us how to study scripture on our own. I can remember Ethel saying as I was preparing for my first year of college: "Now it's your turn to lead a Bible study, Becky." I gulped, but her suggestion that I pray about it inspired me to be on the lookout for the people God would give me.

The Renwicks believed that most Evangelicals tend to flock to the same church, often leaving more liberal congregations devoid of vibrant, committed Evangelicals. They themselves found mainline churches full of open and spiritually hungry people. Ethel told of one example: "I recall meeting a woman for lunch who was a pillar of the church. We talked about programs and organizational details. But on the way home, she began pouring out her personal problems. After we had discussed them, I simply said, 'Let's pray about this. The Lord cares so much about you. He'll show us the way for you. She looked at me in stunned silence, then said, 'No one has ever prayed for me before.' The woman began to weep. She had gone to church all her life, yet she had never realized that Jesus was alive and personal, that Christ could live in us and love us and guide us."

"If only Christians could see the power they have in the Holy Spirit," Ethel says. "We are small and weak. But God himself lives in us! And he will multiply what we do. We may be only one small pebble in a pond, but that one plunk of obedience causes motion in the rest of the water. God multiplies what we do!"

Hazel Offner, a woman who has also shaped my life and has had a profound impact through her Bible study leadership in the Champaign-Urbana area, says of Ethel: "I have never met anyone who so stretched my vision. Together, we drew up a chart of my neighborhood and prayed for each family by name. We wrote down the names of people in the neighborhood and prayed for each family by name. We wrote down the names of people in the Presbyterian church whom Ethel had just met and prayed for them. Ethel had never met my neighbors, and I had never met her Presbyterian friends, but, together, we believed God to accomplish great things in them and in us as we prayed. The result for me was a neighborhood Bible study which turned into an all-community study of forty-five small groups. My life—and my understanding of God—was never the same again.

"Ethel's faith was contagious. There wasn't any dream too big for her to dream and to believe that God would cause to become reality. She knew that there was marvelous untapped potential in everyone around her, and she was so expectant—both before God in prayer and demonstrably to the persons themselves as her soul touched theirs—that it was impossible not to catch her faith and her vision and to become expectant, too. She seldom expressed negative feelings; rather, there was constant, pervasive expectancy that God was just waiting and was eager to change and use people. I can recall several times when a name would come to her as we were talking and she would interrupt the conversation for a moment and spontaneously lift that person to God. By the time she left Champaign, after two years there, one life after another had been deeply affected and changed by God."

When Ethel and Frank returned to Arizona, where she now lives, she worked at the International Food Bazaar, managing fourteen kitchens representing nine different nationalities. Her knowledge of international cuisines stood her in good stead—and so did her knowledge of people. "Waitresses and busboys would ask me if we could talk. They told me they were addicted to drugs and wanted to stop. They asked for my help." Ethel would listen intently to convey a genuine concern as well as God's love for each person. She also invited a guest speaker, a physician, to lecture to the entire staff on why drugs led only to a dead end. And she regularly scheduled Christian speakers who had been on drugs themselves to come and speak to the staff on various subjects, including faith in Christ.

As she recounted this story, I marvelled at the thought of teenagers admitting such a problem to their boss. After all, she could have fired them. But they sensed that they could trust her. Such trust says a great deal about Ethel, but she insists that it says much more about God. "It's Jesus in me that enabled me to see pain I might otherwise have missed. He gives us a love that truly comes from above. If you'd told me in college that I would love a drug addict much less know one—I would have been amazed." "But when God lives in you, what draws you into people's lives isn't duty or social work, it's his love that keeps penetrating the barrier," she says.

Part of her sensitivity to pain comes from the presence of God in her life and part comes from firsthand experience. Throughout the years, her life has been marked by pain as well as privilege.

Several of her close friends have suffered from alcoholism. She has cleaned up after them, held them, and provided hour-to-hour emotional support as well as physical nurture. She has had the painful experience of telling some that they were addicted to alcohol and needed professional help, only to be avoided by them from that time on.

Her own family suffered tragic automobile accidents, serious physical problems, and other crushing blows, resulting in the premature deaths of three of her five brothers and sisters. Perhaps her deepest grief has been over the death of her husband Frank.

In a way that only God could order, I was home one night, contrary to my previous expectations, when George Renwick called me with the sad news that his father was gravely ill. Abruptly, George said, "Becky, call mother, right now, please." I hung up, dialed, and Ethel answered, having been informed only seconds before that her husband had died.

Later, she said, "There are so many stages one goes through with the death of a spouse. At first, I felt that half of me had died. My major human support was buried. Nothing else seemed to matter. I felt I had no place, no mooring, apart from the constancy of God's love and the comfort of my children. Six months later the phone would ring, and I would begin immediately to recount in my mind all that I wanted to tell Frank. As I leapt to the receiver, I would remember that he was gone. It's hard to describe just how deeply the loss of someone you love can affect you. But as I received God's love, as well as the tremendous care of my children and friends, I began to be healed. The numbness started to leave."

One of the friends to offer comfort was Corrie ten Boom. It was a remarkable experience for me to sit in a living room with Ethel, her sister Adele, her three children, and Corrie. It was obvious that Corrie loved Ethel and knew only too well the pain that comes from the death of a loved one. But her eyes shone as she said in her heavy Dutch accent, "My dear sister, vee don't vant him back. Frank ist vith our Jesus now! *Think* of it."

After the initial pain, Ethel experienced yet another level of grief. "I had to deal with my new social status. People treated me differently as a widow. I was no longer invited to all the social gatherings that I had been. Businesses did not take me as seriously. A male voice on the telephone carries more clout, I discovered, than a female voice. So I had to learn to deal with that.

"The third, unexpected stage of recovery happened when God gave me a new ministry. My book on nutrition *Let's Eat Real Food* was published in 1977 and is now in its eighth edition (Grand Rapids: Zondervan). I began leading seminars for individual Christians as well as for schools and secular groups, teaching others how to eat sensibly and responsibly. After that, all kinds of opportunities opened up."

All kinds of opportunities, indeed! One week before I flew to Arizona to interview her, I was speaking at a conference in

Pennsylvania. As I was autographing books, a woman came up to me and said, "I couldn't believe you mentioned Ethel Renwick in the foreword to your book. She changed your life spiritually and my life physically. My family suffered from headaches, hypoglycemia, and poor eating habits. Reading her book changed our eating patterns. We feel like new people. We keep her book on our coffee table and have given copies to our friends."

In short, there is life after tragedy and loss. "Sorrow," relates Ethel, "is God's greatest opportunity to deal with us. Because in those times we are so defenseless. We know that we simply cannot continue on our own. We can't heal ourselves or fill the gap. But God can meet us on our knees. He can have deeper access to us in our pain. And he does heal the brokenhearted and bind up their wounds."

What exactly is her present ministry? "In many ways, I believe God has taken all the strands of my life and made them come together, to do what he called me to now," she says.

Perhaps a story will best illustrate. I told the Lord as I fell asleep in Ethel's apartment on the night of my interview with her that I wanted to convey the depth and significance of what she does. I was awakened early the next morning by a telephone call for Ethel. It was from a woman who had recently brought a friend to see Ethel. The friend had attempted suicide twice. Ethel had spent four hours listening to her spill out her problems. Ethel asked her spiritual questions, but she also inquired about her eating and drinking habits. It became clear that in addition to being emotionally and spiritually troubled, she was also a physical wreck. She was living on colas and valium.

So Ethel suggested that this young woman change her eating patterns and begin filling her body with nutritious foods. She told her that God cared for her physically and emotionally as well as spiritually. If she wanted real health, in every dimension, she needed to be invaded by God through Jesus Christ. It was clear that the distraught woman was moved, almost astonished by the kind of God who loved every part of her. She had never heard the Gospel presented in such an integrated way. She thought Christianity was just for the soul. She had not realized that God made provision for every dimension of life—body and soul. He wanted her to be whole and she knew she was fragmented. She left, saying she was determined to change her physical habits and to seek God as well.

That morning's telephone call related the news that the troubled woman was on the road to physical recovery and spiritual renewal. For the first time, she felt hope and not despair. Ironically, the person telephoning with the good news had, herself, gone to Ethel only months before with many of the same problems: suicidal, addicted to valium. Through Ethel's help, she, too, rededicated her life to Jesus Christ.

Says Ethel: "We say we're concerned about wholeness as Christians, yet we so often avoid the physical dimension. The only thing that nourishes the brain and the nervous system is food. Yet it never occurs to us to check what a depressed person has been eating, as one indication of the source of the problem. Food affects how we see the world. It can make our minds clear or fuzzy. If we load our bodies with sugar and caffeine, we get a lift only to crash later. How can we be a vital witness to God? God wants his children to be strong and healthy and clear-minded—not addicts."

How did Ethel's ministry come to include a concern for people's physical well-being? "It was because I kept meeting people who didn't feel well. It was especially alarming how many of them were Christians who told me they were tired, with little energy and feeling depressed." They often felt the culprit was spiritual inadequacy. As Ethel questioned them about their diet she was disheartened by how poorly they ate. They cared deeply about the Kingdom, yet they ignored and even abused the vessel God works through to build his Kingdom—our bodies."

In our nation's diet, Ethel warns, "we eat more candy than eggs, more sugar than vegetables, fruits, and eggs combined; we drink more soft drinks than milk. And since 1971, we eat more processed foods than fresh foods. We send our children off to school carrying a lunch box filled with a sandwich made of fluffy enriched white bread, potato chips and a couple of cookies, not even stopping to think what ingredients or chemicals are in those basic ingredients. We often reward children with destructive food, and then we wonder why they seem so high-strung and irritable. We have bake sales at church to raise money for the poor by selling impoverished, nutrient-less food."

Strong words? Then hear what she has to say about Christians!

"The Lord recently sent me someone who loves him—a pastor's wife—who was in great need. Her story is the same I hear from so many—unexplained anxiety, depression, fatigue, increased mental problems. The doctors after many tests, found nothing wrong with her. Yet her diet was atrocious! (but very usual)."

Ethel believes that our ignorance of today's food has serious consequences and that Christians are especially accountable for these consequences. Her latest book, *Feeding the Faithful* (Keats Publishing), rises out of just this conviction. From the book she writes, "There has been a radical departure in many ways from the food which God designed for our bodies and the food we accept today with little question. . . . Perhaps one reason that scripture mentions eating and drinking to the glory of God is because, when we disobey this, we self-destruct to some degree; we are less than we could be for Him."

The strands have, indeed, come together—personal commitment to Christ, energetic witness in the world, the understanding of the relationship between physical and spiritual well-being. Through her life, Ethel has provided an example of tireless dedication and caring love to countless individuals. Hers is an example that merits close examination.

The underlying assumption of this book is that in addition to needing heroes and role-models we must be ones for others.

Ours is a strange age. Never have we hungered more for heroes or tried so hard to defame them. We lived through the nightmare of Watergate, but it has left us more cynical than before. Nevertheless, we still ache for heroes, even if we are no longer comfortable with them. Pete Dawkins, all-American football player, Rhodes scholar, the most luminous graduate of West Point, and now, at age forty-three, the youngest general in the U.S. Army, said in an interview with my husband, Wesley: "A lot of things that are central parts of our lives are transcendent or abstract. But it's hard for us to deal with courage or dedication or sacrifice in the abstract.

We need to have people who embody those qualities, who are reassuring and real. What we really want is to believe in people." Yet we live in an age of the "anti-hero." As Hawkins says, "We seem to turn on our's [heroes] with special fervor, driven by an almost compulsive need to scratch and rub anyone of heroic dimension until we find a wart or flaw. We microscopically examine people in public life until we find something about them that is flawed."

Yet the human heart cannot seem to resist the desire to elevate someone above the masses: whether this tendency is realized in the exuberant outpouring of joy and enthusiasm for the Pope; the poignant scene where hundreds kept vigil outside Yoko Ono's home the night John Lennon was slain, or the wearing of hideous T-shirts for Gary Gilmore or Claus van Bulow. As disparate as these examples are, we must listen to what our culture is telling us. We need heroes. People want to believe in someone.

We must distinguish between *celebrities* and *heroes.* Never be ashamed of having a hero or of being one. But be leery of the celebrity-mania that exists in America today. There will always be an abundance of celebrities, but there is a paucity of genuine heroes in the land.

Garry Trudeau, the creator of the comic strip "Doonesbury," spoke of this in his 1981 commencement address at Colby College: "This is a deeply cynical age where generosity is in short supply. You will find that this technological society will soon reveal its limitations. It is a world where taking a stand has come to mean finding the nearest trap door for escape. . . . You will find that your worth is measured not by what you are, but by how you are perceived. There is something disturbing in our society when men wish not to be esteemed, but to be envied. . . . When that happens, God help us."

A popular television show was being broadcast in the nation's capital, just the kind of thing that Washington loves best: top news men and women questioning a news-making political celebrity. Senator Barry Goldwater was an exceptionally good guest that night. His answers were characteristically tough, feisty, and candid. As the program came to a close, one interviewer said, "We always ask this, sir, in the last thirty seconds, realizing it's not nearly as significant as the other things we've discussed, but who has been the greatest influence in your life? Who has been one of your heroes?" There was silence. One by one each reporter looked up. The silence became awkward. The camera zoomed in for a close-up and the reason for the silence became immediately apparent. Senator Goldwater was fighting back his emotions. His voice breaking, he apologized to the startled reporters.

Finally he said, "It's a man you've probably never heard of. I'm sure he himself had no idea the impact he made on me as a young man. But he modeled for me all the things I've ever aspired to be. He pointed me in the right direction. He believed in me and he cared for me. He was a great man."

That night a politically powerful man wept publically on television. Not because he won an election, or lost an election, or was indicted (as is too often the case!). He wept because he had a hero. That night I realized that Senator Goldwater and I have a great deal in common. The thought of my hero also makes me weep.

CHRISTIAN HERALD ASSOCIATION AND ITS MINISTRIES

CHRISTIAN HERALD ASSOCIATION, founded in 1878, publishes The Christian Herald Magazine, one of the leading interdenominational religious monthlies in America. Through its wide circulation, it brings inspiring articles and the latest news of religious developments to many families. From the magazine's pages came the initiative for CHRISTIAN HERALD CHILDREN and THE BOWERY MISSION, two individually supported not-for-profit corporations.

CHRISTIAN HERALD CHILDREN, established in 1894, is the name for a unique and dynamic ministry to disadvantaged children, offering hope and opportunities which would not otherwise be available for reasons of poverty and neglect. The goal is to develop each child's potential and to demonstrate Christian compassion and understanding to children in need.

Mont Lawn is a permanent camp located in Bushkill, Pennsylvania. It is the focal point of a ministry which provides a healthful "vacation with a purpose" to children who without it would be confined to the streets of the city. Up to 1000 children between the age of 7 and 11 come to Mont Lawn each year.

Christian Herald Children maintains year-round contact with children by means of a *City Youth Ministry.* Central to its philosophy is the belief that only through sustained relationships and demonstrated concern can individual lives be truly enriched. Special emphasis is on individual guidance, spiritual and family counseling and tutoring. This follow-up ministry to inner-city children culminates for many in financial assistance toward higher education and career counseling.

THE BOWERY MISSION, located at 227 Bowery, New York City, has since 1879 been reaching out to the lost men on the Bowery, offering them what could be their last chance to rebuild their lives. Every man is fed, clothed and ministered to. Countless numbers have entered the 90-day residential rehabilitation program at the Bowery Mission. A concentrated ministry of counseling, medical care, nutrition therapy, Bible study and Gospel services awakens a man to spiritual renewal within himself.

These ministries are supported solely by the voluntary contributions of individuals and by legacies and bequests. Contributions are tax deductible. Checks should be made out either to CHRISTIAN HERALD CHILDREN or to THE BOWERY MISSION.

Administrative Office: 40 Overlook Drive, Chappaqua, New York 10514
Telephone: (914) 769-9000